The Worst Council

By Henry Vietski

Contents

The Worst Council 1

Dedication 6

Introduction 15

The Big Picture...34

Micro managed society 42

Agenda 21..44

Agenda 2030..45

Climate change action..49

Government 'shut the f up program' 53

The Corporation 55

Journey into Local Government 57

Local Governments that believe in the snake oil
salesman..60

The main differences between local government and
the private sector..62

One Glaring Omission...63

The Banished Manager and Jackie Sackem.............64

The incompetent manager 69

Ranger Wars...72

Roundup questions 75

The regional 'open cheque book' project.................78

Compaction woes...87

Acceptance woes 91

Sub prime slackers..95

Finance rogue 99

You've got mail...100

Grudge holders incorporated...............................102

To my haters 104

Council workers sacked 106

Selecting the right candidate ? 108

Fees and charges?...111

What happens when the assets are all sold?.........113

Rates increases 116

Widening pay gaps...119

The dictatorship...121

A solution? 123

Experiences of some others...............................125

One resident's subdivision nightmare...................128

Other Municipalities...129

The worst of it...132

Complaints to local governments 134

How does your Council perform? 137

Smile, you're on camera....................................138

Believe you can make a difference 139

The End 140

References 141

About the Author 149

Dedication

I have often been inspired to write.

This is one of those occasions.

Every time I have written a book, there always been a motivating factor, an underlying urge to have my say about something.

Mostly it has been with the intent of helping people to better understand the world we live in, along with my own thoughts regarding how to improve things.

This time, however, I have another motivating force.

I am hoping that this book will be the best, most thought provoking written work I have ever put together, but also that it will help generate some more interest and involvement in local municipalities in general.

I thought about a less provocative title but then reverted back to the original.

I am not saying all Local Governments are bad, but there are more than a few that aren't great.

Whilst writing this book, I was reminded that things aren't so bad here in the developed world.

In comparison to the state of affairs in some places, on the surface there's really not much to complain about.

Here I am about to have a whine about some of the exasperating issues I have faced whilst working in a relatively free country, for a variety of local government organisations.

Even if this work is trivial in the big scheme of things, it is also significant, in that it is a testament to the fact that we do still live in a relatively free nation, evidenced by the fact that you are able to read this book.

In some countries, writers have been thrown in jail for speaking their mind, especially when it relates to criticism of their government, even if it's constructive and factual.

At the extreme end of things, in recent times we have seen what happened to the likes of Edward Snowden and Julian Assange, but across the world there are many more examples of folk who have said something that their government didn't like and they have been targeted as a result.

So I am exercising my right and privilege that I have as a citizen of a free country to have my say, even if in the big scheme of things it's relatively trivial, we should all be thankful that I can not only have an opinion, but the right to express it as well.

I am grateful for having the privilege of being able to say what I think and perhaps because of that I am keenly aware that if we do not cherish and protect the right to free speech it may be lost forever. It must be defended, and I believe one of the key points that must be made to those in power is that freedom of speech is a sign of a mature society.

Of course there have been a lot of assaults on the right to free speech as well, under new hate crime legislation, but largely that is concentrated on those that incite violence, and I am quite the opposite in that I believe we need an end to violence.

To put into perspective and contrast with what our ancestors put up with, we are quite lucky to be living in this day and age, but increasingly there are examples across the world of how our right to free speech is in a precarious situation, and the reason I thought I should mention it in this book.

The fact is, you cannot force anyone to believe anything that they don't want to believe.

If they are forbidden from expressing their view then it will persist.

Perhaps though that there are some falsehoods that have been so completed integrated into our society that to question them would cause a significant change in our world.

In the developed nations across the world today, most people have living standards that would be unimaginable luxury compared to that only a few generations ago.

We don't even have to go back hundreds of years to find a stark contrast between society today and the hardships our recent ancestors had to endure.

My Grampa for example, started out by fleeing Warsaw when the Nazis invaded Poland.

He was eventually captured on his trek west and was put on a train and sent to work on a Farm in France as slave labour.

Freezing winters sleeping in a barn and near starvation he had to endure as a boy when he was only 13 or 14 years old.

I believe that the French resistance helped secure his escape, if I remember the story correctly, he escaped just before the Nazis started rounding the labour up and machine gunning them before the Allies arrived.

After the war he went to Scotland where he met my Nanna.

I didn't get back home in time to see my Nanna again before she passed away, I was really hoping to get a better paying job so that I could afford to take my family to meet her, but I didn't even get an interview for the job I was probably most qualified to do it and had been waiting patiently for the vacancy to come up.

Whilst I can't prove it, when I started investigating I found out that there was a very strong possibility that a previous bullying little ego maniac boss had effectively stuck the boots in and stopped me from getting the job I applied for.

The man didn't even have the cajonies to tell me what his problem was with me, always preferring to take the sneaky approach by bad mouthing me to others.

Presumably he wasn't that bright either, since some of the people he spoke to about me were friends of mine.

Or maybe he was a passive aggressive, quite a contrast to another boss I once had who saw himself as samurai sword wielding silverback, but even he was not up there with one of the bosses I had who was so bad that a colleague of mine once referred to him as bad as Vlad the Impaler. He went on to add that he wouldn't be surprised to see his victims strung up around the perimeter of his domain.

The reason I mention it is because even in infuriating situations there are always ways to see the upside.

For example, that pea brained muppet that had stopped me from getting that job that I had been waiting for a decade to apply for, pissed me off so much that it's given me enough inspiration to write this book.

As anyone knows who has written a book will testify, it's not that easy to do without sufficient motivation, but when there's some emotion involved it's probably also a good point to remind myself not to overdo it. I wouldn't want to sound like a whinger.

Another example of being able to see the upside comes from a story my Grampa once told me.

When he was a boy he lived in Warsaw and when the Nazis invaded, his Mother gave all her money to her children and told them to flee the City. He was captured and endured all sorts of hardships whist being forced to work for the Nazis on a farm in France. He didn't talk about it often, probably the most common story he did tell was over one Christmas where he was hungry and cold, and a Nazi soldier gave him an apple, which helped restore his faith in humanity – even amongst the ranks of the Nazis.

Presumably my Grampa's experiences gave him more appreciation for life and consideration of others to such extent that he would do things like go up the hill in winter and feed the birds.

He was a kind and generous man, and I have no doubt that he was a big influence to selfish me as a youngster, in showing me that there was always consideration of others.

One of the things that he always seemed overly concerned with was whether I was cold in the winter, which only really made sense once I had heard his story about his experiences, but perhaps it may have been also after our experience one night when we went night fishing off the pier in Deal. That night was cold, and after telling Grampa I was cold, he gave me his jacket to stay warm.

We pulled in fluorescent seaweed and more than a few crabs that night, it was only later on that I discovered that there was a nuclear power plant near where we were fishing.

My Grampa gave me the motivation to take the plunge and move to Australia as well, he reminded me that life is short and that "you will only know if you give it a go."

Perhaps giving it a go is something that runs in the family. I also remember my Grampa telling me that the family name was part of a group of polish noble families. The main difference between Polish nobility and English was that most of the Polish nobility had earned their status by their deeds, and the origins of the family status as a szlachta clan was from some outnumbered farmers repelling a barbarian invasion.

He also told me that all who shared the same family name were related.

So I was fascinated to also hear the story of another famous bloke with the same family name, who had been a Polish naval officer at the outbreak of WW2.

It turns out that this guy was a top gun U Boat hunter. He was so good he ended up being given a ship from the British navy to help the allies.

Some of his logs included making convoy runs along the North Sea, in weather which included 30 metre swells in icy waters with convoys of dozens of ships.

Unfortunately he eventually got torpedoed, but not before he had taken out a long list of U-Boats.

So I dedicate this book to my Grampa, my Nanna, my Mum and Dad, my brother and his family, my Aunts, Uncles, Cousins, second Cousins and to my other half and our children, my friends, and everyone else I know.

We all have our own unique stories to tell and I encourage everyone to get theirs in print as well, even if you self publish it, it will stand both as a snapshot in time, and provide a small piece of the tapestry of life in this world in the early part of the 21st Century.

As I have found, more reading writing also has enabled me to explore strange new worlds and now that I can comfortably write a book, I also have come to realise that it is the one thing that a writer has and that is the ability to steer the story in any direction.

Although I have endured trials and tribulations for many years in my own working life, I have also considered the possibility of one of the reasons perhaps I enjoy writing so much is because there is an environment where I am in total control of it.

Maybe that is a bit of escapism on my behalf, but it has become more than a hobby, since I generally write something every day.

I suppose these days many people write something every day, on social media platforms.

I suppose that escapism is what must be a driving force for many authors who write fiction.

Anyway I hope it's an enjoyable read and it's always good to hear some feedback, so feel free to let me know what you think once you have read this book, you can email me at henry.vietski@mail.com

Cheers

H

Introduction

This book is largely a first-hand account of some of my experiences working for a range of local governments, over a 20 year period.

I have also included some related local government stories that have appeared in the news in recent years throughout the book.

If I was at an interview and someone asked me why I wanted to work for local government, I would probably say it was because I get to work in my chosen field of expertise and also there is such a great diversity of things that local governments are involved in, there is constant communication with local residents and there is always action, it's interesting and challenging.

Blah, blah blah.

To my friends, I might summarise it a bit more succinctly by saying :

"What a ride into crazy town it has been."

In every single local government I have worked for, I have left feeling I was somewhat mistreated, even when I factor in my own contributing actions which lead to it, one thing I do have is a strong sense of justice.

I am all too aware that people make mistakes, the wrong decisions and generally stuff things up from time to time, we are only human after all, and I try to be quick to forgive, but unfortunately I have found that it isn't always reciprocated.

Many folk seem to be petty minded and content with their own selfish perspective and seem to find it difficult to empathise with others.

I may also have been a bit like that myself in the past, but less so these days, particularly with my improved understanding of the tools of the emerging Orwellian society.

Perhaps that's not something which is exclusively found within the realm of local government, but a broader statement about society in general.

We are all so engrossed in our own gadgets and the latest technology, toys and gizmos that increasingly and ironically, as technology connects everyone more completely, the general public seem increasingly subject to zombification and are oblivious to their immediate surroundings.

I wonder, for example how many people have been run over by a car because they were walking along text messaging someone and not paying attention.

So if people aren't even aware of their surroundings when walking up the road, what chance is there of them becoming interested let alone active in relation to affairs of their local municipality?

Few people read these days and current affairs in general are of less interest to most folk than watching cute kittens or playful puppies frolicking in video clips.

Most people of course think that they stay up to date with current affairs because they watch the news on the television, or read the newspaper, but then most pay more attention to the sports section or the other trivia that accompanies it.

Of course the major corporate media networks have been severely consolidated in recent times, and they have worked very hard on trying to demonise critical thinkers.

Most of the time, the individuals hailed as 'free thinkers' by the corporate media are actually just good teleprompter readers, parroting the view given to them by their corporate masters.

Conspiracy theorists are now in the same basket as 'extremists' even if they aren't violent, according to the corporate whores on the telly.

'Fake news' is the new label applied to alternative and independent media in the corporate media's attempt to steer people away from news and views that stray from the official narrative.

In the face of such baloney as 'babies in incubators' and other pure fiction peddled as truth by the mainstream media, more and more people are alert to who is peddling the fake news around the place.

The local media usually have a keen eye on local government affairs and one way or another there is usually plenty of interaction between the two.

Local radio networks are often keenly interested in goings on at their local council, and sometimes it's a spontaneous thing, when a person calls in and explains their issue, and then the next thing they have the Mayor on the radio.

An example of this was when a local Council decided to purchase a Mercedes Benz for the Mayor. Whilst the purchase may have made sense financially in terms of whole of life costs compared to something more traditional, someone should have given some thought to what the perception and subsequent backlash might have been before going ahead with it. The media made a meal out of that one.

In my time working for local government I have seen both the good and the bad in terms of relationships between the local press and the council.

Many local papers send their journalists to attend Council meetings.

In most local governments, there is usually an authorised public relations specialist, and with the exception of senior staff such as the Chief Executive and the appointed media spokesperson, staff are generally not permitted to talk to the media.

Increasingly, elected members are also required to sign documentation once they have been elected, this is usually a code of conduct related document.

I will preface what I am going to say by saying that local municipalities around the world vary somewhat, and I have only experienced working for them in two nations – both of them developed countries.

Even locally, there are likely vast differences between municipality, with the good, the bad and the ugly.

I wonder what percent are in each category across my own State.

If there was an award for the worst council, there would likely be a long list of candidates as evidenced throughout this book, although I would also highlight the fact that any local government can change rapidly, either for the better or worse, as staff and elected members change.

The stories in here are all snapshots in time, and whilst most of the stories I have mentioned have happened in recent years, some as recently as early 2017, but others go back to the 1990's and this point is worth highlighting because perhaps by the time you have read any one of the following stories there could have been a complete change in the organisation.

Don't hold your breath though, as often senior management take their cronies with them when they move jobs and form their own little gang of untouchables.

I will leave it up to you to determine whether or not your own municipality has got better or worse.

You are the customer and at the end of the day, it is the customer who determines whether or not the quality of service is up to par or not.

I have communicated my concerns regarding the current state of affairs to Ministers on all sorts of issues of national significance, and issues relating to the State and locally, as it's everyone's duty to care about the future of the nation, to be a part of helping to shape it into something that we do want.

By having some input into the political process and expressing our views, we have some say in our future.

On a local level, however we probably all could be doing bit more participating or at least informing ourselves on a more regular basis as to what's going on.

That's quite easy to do on one level, because Council meetings are usually recorded and minutes these days are often available soon after the meetings have taken place.

Many people don't even know that there are opportunities to attend Council meetings and ask questions, although anyone thinking of doing so should check, since many have policies that they want to know in advance if you are going to raise a specific question.

At least then they have some time to bring along any relevant information when the meeting takes place.

As I see it there are a variety of vulnerabilities in our current system of Government and at all levels.

Apart from the number of governments that have become fiscally unsustainable, there are other vulnerabilities that have the potential to produce less than favourable outcomes for us, the general public.

I have always said if I am wrong about creeping tyranny then so be it, but liberty needs to be watched with eagle eyes, as a society we need to be concerned with it and put into place safeguards to prevent any inadvertent or deliberate steps to erode it, for the sake of future generations.

There seems to be too much apathy and ignorance amongst the general populace; perhaps that's changing, albeit slowly.

The world today is so interconnected that any number of things could cause major disruption.

We need independence, not interdependence.

For example, a global financial meltdown would likely cause chaos.

As a hedge against this, Australia could for example have a parallel currency made out of some of those precious metals, a physical coinage.

Having two lots of money is possible, for example in Scotland they accept English money and vice versa.

By having coins we would be preserving at least a bit more of those precious metals, and in the event of a global financial calamity, the relative value of that currency would likely skyrocket as well. It makes total sense, especially when one does a comparison between how much is mined and how much we as a nation currently keep in the vaults.

In some nations, local municipalities run everything including local Police departments and in others, local authorities are limited to maybe road maintenance and waste collections.

I will mention a few notable overseas municipalities towards the end of the book, but other than that, mostly this is about local governments that I have experienced first -hand, in Australia although I have looked at both the UK and USA as well as part of research when writing this book.

From what I have seen, there are some very good systems in place, and whilst some local governments take too long to do things due to cumbersome administrative processes, some of them actually do a good job of 'managing the community'.

Also, I think that many people don't understand that there are sometimes good reasons why things take a long time to process.

For example if a commercial business wants to set up shop, then the business activity has to be considered and ideally the surrounding residents might be consulted.

If it's a polluting industrial process then it's especially important. Also when significant building works are needed, for example, you wouldn't like it if your neighbour put up a block of apartments that blocked out all your sunlight without having been asked about the idea first, for example, if it blocked the view of the ocean.

Whilst local government may be the one with least power compared to State or Federal government, it is the one closest to the people, and for that reason alone, perhaps local government should have more autonomy, since local laws are more likely to suit local situations when they have been enacted in the area to which they apply.

The more remote the source of the rules, the less relevant they are likely to be. At least if a local government makes a decision you don't like, you have access to the people that made the decision since they live in your town.

Having said that, I am not sure that many local governments in their present format would be capable or responsible enough to take on more authority, and certainly from a libertarian viewpoint, we need a reversal in the incrementally increasing intrusion from government in general, in my opinion.

I am not sure where my avid interest in geopolitical affairs comes from, whether it is an inherited or learned behaviour, but I certainly think that having a diverse and world spanning family has made me more aware of the current geopolitical landscape.

I guess my own research has caused me to question everything and upon discovering the extent of the fakery, greed and corruption in the world, like so many others, I have felt compelled to have my say.

I am lucky to have such a large family and with all my cousins and aunts and uncles living in a variety of developed nations around the world including Canada, the UK, the USA, when I think of some of their stories, perhaps a book about one bloke's experience working for a local government is about as appealing as watching paint dry in comparison, so for that reason I will only include some of the most significant 'highlights' and try to keep it entertaining.

One of the reasons it has taken so long to put this book is because I believed that it might result in my ex-communication from ever working for any local government again.

Whilst I am not generally one to hold back, I think it's sad that in this 'free' society that even I often feel that I have to censor what I say lest anyone gets upset about it. If that is typical of someone who makes a conscious effort to say it as I see it, then what chance is there that others do the same?

Many of those guys (and gals) in local government circles talk to each other, they attend the same functions and are affiliated through all sorts of networks and associations.

If you piss the wrong person off, they have the ability to talk shit about you behind your back and as the old saying goes 'if you throw enough of it…'.

However having already broken the vow to never work for a local government ever again, at this point it doesn't concern me in the least.

Think what you like!

I am now free of the oppression I have experienced in local government and don't want to go back there.

I am also reminded that I have also seen the most amazing 'shut the fuck up' program, provided by a different level of government that I once worked for.

I will include that story in its own chapter.

I am not perfect, I have made my fair share of stuff-ups, made the wrong decisions or taken the wrong approach managing staff, but I have always fought for the teams that I have been responsible for and at least I have learned from mistakes, or at least I have tried to.

Another way of saying it might be that I woke up and opened my eyes to the world around me and in my efforts to wake up others, have been black marked for my relatively outspoken views.

I have tried every approach possible that have been limited only by my own creativity.

Shouting from the roof tops about issues one is concerned with doesn't work, people just start thinking you are crazy. (No doubt helped along by the perception managers over at mainstream media.)

But sometimes, even more subtle approaches can cause retaliation.

I have found myself that some have been effectively programmed to such a great extent that they will go beyond just taking a dislike to what I believe.

It's like they have been programmed to attack. Perhaps it's a result of MK-Ultra. So many zombies!

It's not nice, but it is an unfortunate reality for those who dare to think outside the box, and then speak their mind, that it gets held against them as though it's a bad thing.

I guess the main reason is that when discussing world views, people generally don't want to know that it's all bullshit, the pure fiction we get from the mainstream media.

They don't want to know about it because to acknowledge it would require some effort on their part.

Also the middle class tend to be more closed minded compared to the working class, presumably because the workers are at the pointy end of the stick.

Plenty of folk walk around pretending everything is sweet in the world with a nice big house, car and family earning big bucks.

Why would they want to listen to some opinionated Council worker who wants some effort spent on protecting their freedoms?

People have told me, get on with your own life, don't worry about there's nothing you can do, it's just how it is. I am getting on with my life, and wanting to improve on the current state of affairs has to be a worthy cause.

Also it's not all bad; I have had plenty of supportive comments from people as well, sometimes from those who think the same but prefer not to speak of it.

Yes it's a tough job but someone has to do it, because more time needs to be spent discussing issues that matter and not something that doesn't like the footy results.

See that's another example right there, footy.

In Australia its almost sacrilege to express an opinion which doesn't bow at the altar of footy, or soccer, or basketball, or whatever it is that we get so distracted with, I have had people take a dislike to me for daring to suggest that the modern day bread and circuses are a giant distraction while the world managers continue on pushing ahead with their totalitarian one world government plans.

I get it, I know what it's like looking forward to a sports event, and know that if there's a screen in front of me I will likely get absorbed by it too, but I just want more people to think more about the important things as well, and don't hate me just because I don't follow a footy team.

If I have consistently made one mistake, it's been being too transparent, like the night I explained why I didn't follow the footy whilst at a pub.

People have used that against me in many ways.

I have trodden on enough toes at sufficiently high level for it to have undoubtedly have had a negative effect on my career.

It's bad enough being a creative innovative pioneering type within the confines of slow bureaucratic administrative processes, without having the boss also lining up the crosshairs.

I do think that there are probably a reasonably large number of people who would be interested in knowing the perspective from someone who has worked for local municipalities, regardless of whether they work for one or not.

Whilst I am not saying it applies to all Councils, I know quite a few other people who have been exasperated by their apparently inhumane treatment at the hands of 'the machine' which is usually ironic because most local governments do proclaim to be bastions of fair treatment.

I love writing and I think I am getting better at it.

I don't get the time like I used to devote to writing, but I make up for it in the quantity I can churn out when I do sit down to write. This book will no doubt be finished in record time.

The first time I tried publishing a book, I used a publisher to do it all, the front cover, the formatting and printing. That took about 2 years including writing it.

The next book I wrote, also took about 2 years, but I only got someone to format it and do the book cover.

The next book I put together was a collection of a great deal of other written work I had put together over a 5 year period. That also took 2 years, but I did everything myself including the formatting and front cover.

Now I am familiar with the book producing process, I am expecting to have the first draft ready to proof read in a matter of weeks.

Hopefully the quality is reasonable enough.

I am well used to putting out written work, I had a blog which at its peak got me over 20,000 views on a single article and at the peak of my blogging, I once posted almost daily with up to a couple of thousand words per article.

I usually find myself writing about something, whether it's fiction or non-fiction, which I think is a good thing, since it seems to use a part of the brain that is different from say calculating finances.

I have recently been widening the field of my written works and I have multiple written projects running concurrently.

I always seem to find myself commenting on a wide range of issues relating to the world we live in, it doesn't seem to matter where the conversation starts out, that's where it goes to, almost always, although I am more mindful these days that it's better to not go on too much about any one thing for too long.

It's largely because I actually do care about the world we live in, but I have not been shy about having my say, my two cents worth, mainly in an attempt to help us make the future a better place.

I have rattled a few cages in the process but being a fan of continuous improvement, perhaps these days I am slightly better at diplomacy than perhaps in the past.

I have an interest in the state of affairs from a worldwide perspective, and one of the minorities that has dared to express an opinion that sometimes differs from the views that the corporate media would rather you held.

To express such views in this day and age can be somewhat like trying to navigate through a minefield of political correctness in which you better watch out lest some fragile self-proclaimed social justice warrior gets their knickers in a twist.

I can type faster and more accurately now, and that helps get the thoughts into black and white more efficiently, even if some people would prefer I didn't.

However, I am more informed than that lot, because whilst they are watching the footy I am reading up on current affairs.

I wasn't going to write this at all, even after deciding to never go back to local government, but then after so many years of encountering both interest and misconceptions across society in general, along with accurate assessments given to me over the years by various stakeholders, is what caused me to finally write on the subject.

I first thought about some of the stories I could share, and that was initially just a few dot points, one-liners that reminded me of a noteworthy moment.

I doubted I would be able to think of enough content to make it into a book.

I thought that there were a couple of standout memorable things, but largely it would probably be boring and as my better half would tell me:

"No-one wants to read that."

I thought at first to check and see, so I began to write the main points, which I put into a list.

It wasn't long before I had expanded the list into dot points with headings for each, which I then made a few more detailed comments.

Before I knew it, in a matter of a few days, I had the outline of a book, about 40 pages in total, and realised that there was more than enough content to fill a book and looking through the list it didn't see quite so boring as one might first think.

All of what I am about to share really happened, albeit from my own perspective.

The events really happened, whilst employed across a number of different local government organisations, spanning a few decades.

I will really try my best to not point out any single individual or organisation in an identifiable way, because that isn't what this book is about, although if it does the so be it , it's in the realm of public interest and true from my own recollections, 100 percent.

The point I would also like to make in this book, is that the floggings will continue until we do something about it, we need to exert political pressure to make change for the better, to become more interested in how we are governed and so on, and the first step is to at least think about these things.

The best I could hope for with this book is that it at least helps in some way to generate further discussion around some of the issues mentioned here.

If it doesn't then that's ok, because I have space on my bookshelf for it and it's at least a summary of my time working in local government.

As I have come to appreciate as I have got older, books endure, they are sometimes timeless and as we see from the likes of Huxley and Orwell, sometimes prophetic.

I don't believe this will be in that category, but who knows, perhaps this will have more relevance in the future than today, but at least I appreciate now that what I write here today, will almost certainly outlast me.

If nothing else I hope it helps add to the general discussion about where we, are as a society heading, and if not, then well at least I am a testament to the fact that in the early part of the 21st Century that there were actually lots of people who had any interest at all in geopolitical affairs.

The Big Picture

In Australia, we broadly have three levels of government, Federal, State and Local and in a nutshell, if we keep continuing to allow international decrees to dictate down to the local level then tyranny is upon us.

I don't actually think that the planned tyranny will succeed, since too many people are now informed and vocal and active in derailing it, peacefully, partly by using the technological tools given to us by the ruling class.

It is a slow process, and as we have seen in recent times, with the Brexit vote (you didn't think that the globalists would relinquish their totalitarian dream without a fight though did you?) and the election of Donald Trump in the USA, the rise of UKIP in the UK and One Nation party in Australia, these are all I believe signs that the people have had enough of the current two party dominated politics across the world, and we will be seeing more of this in the future.

The rise of the independents in politics was something I predicted about five years ahead of it happening, although having said that I have made plenty of other predictions that haven't happened.

The ruling classes and even the current major political parties are no doubt aware of the current public approval ratings at any one time, and know that their only option is to work on continuous improvement both in their approach and outcomes, if they are to retain any chances of staying in power into the future.

I know I am going a little bit off track with local government, but I have a better handle on what's driving international policies than most people I know, so it would be remiss of me to not set the scene of government in broader context before delving into my own reality within a government department.

The Federal Government is being guided via United Nations derived policies that have been leading us into a de facto World Government.

Federal pushes it on to the State and the State passes it on at a local level.

Speak up and have your say or we are all doomed.

Safeguards can be incorporated into agreements and so on in order to protect the future generations of the nation.

Our currently political system is vulnerable to influence from outside forces be it from the corporate or governance sector and so it is always going to be necessary to have scrutiny regarding policies that affect us all, and a better job of it needs to be done than what we have had thus far.

I have tried to be an agent of change for the better using the Freedom Force International creed of 'don't fight city hall, be city hall' although in my case that has been as always to promote more attention to those things that do matter in this world.

In my opinion, clearly the best way to enable our society to avert a disaster in which we descend into a 2 tier class system of the haves and the have nots, or the super-rich and the super-poor, is to keep everyone up to speed with where things are at, and from there, hopefully enough interest and attention will be placed where it needs to go.

At the moment, we are in big danger because the distraction levels are at all-time highs, and that is likely to continue into the future.

Some people will take the piss no matter what happens, and the self-proclaimed elite of this world have spent lots of cash scrutinising populations for the purposes of identifying the best way to enable them to manipulate public opinion.

And manipulate it they have. In my opinion engineered false flag attacks have been used numerous times in recent decades as pretext for furthering the empire's objectives.

Just as they spent years telling lies about WMD's in Iraq and so on, they keep poking Russia with a stick.

I used to think that Edwards Bernays was the pioneer of moulding public opinion, but when we look further back through history and find it really is much older than that.

Local Governments, just like all the other systems of the machine are being either wittingly or unwittingly ushered into a cashless, managed society by the upper echelon, the ruling class.

The ridiculousness of the many eugenicist ego maniacs hell bent on world domination continues, as most of those folk shroud their true nature under a cloak of 'philanthropy' but really they are most interested in depopulation.

A lot of those super wealthy pretenders are probably total psychopaths and they will likely continue to use false flag, engineered events to further their aims.

There are probably more than a few psychos working in local governments as well.

Here we are in the twenty first century and the traditional image of the Council worker leaning on a shovel still endures by many folk.

It's a common thing, when asked 'what do you do?' and I say "I work for Council XYZ".

"Got your own shovel to lean on?"

However this is largely just a perception by people not actually employed by any Council.

Some of the hardest workers I have known have worked for local governments and some of the most decent folk I have ever met also work there.

Over the years I have worked for quite a few Councils and for the most part I have worked alongside some truly great people and made lifelong friends with some of them.

I have experienced some amazing things in local government and in the last few decades I have also seen first-hand the incremental changes that are turning some of them into new world order work camps.

Authoritarianism appears to be marching forwards.

Wasn't it Plato that said democracy turns into despotism?

Welcome to the new world order.

Increasingly, technological tools give rise to the application of increased fines and fees, and the costs just keep on going up and up.

The scientific dictatorship also unfortunately produces increasing numbers of people who are rather less than productive, being ever more concerned with scrutiny and analysis.

The criminalisation of society is all part of the plan it seems, so the plan must change. We have to increase the pressure on the system to enable a more libertarian one.

Privacy is also set to dissolve into oblivion under the current trajectory.

Instead of alphabet agencies and ever increasing fines and penalties, and new departments and taxes and licences and so on, we need less of those things.

It's not going to happen without concerted effort. The rewards are increased productivity and creativity, and of course this reduces budgetary burdens.

The best way to spark an economic boom is to lower taxes.

On another level of course it's all to design, to a planned, managed society, but we won't go there in great depth in this book because that's a whole subject in itself.

Suffice to say that there has been a coordinated effort across the western world to implement global 'harmonization' in policies, driven by various United Nations branches, down to implementation at the local level, where they appear to have been generated locally, but have in effect been handed down by the UN.

That is why so many local authorities in so many nations are all implementing very similar policies.

Take microchipping of pets for example. Once it was option.

Nowadays, one by one, local governments are requiring pets be microchipped.

Oh of course it's so convenient to be able to identify an animal and their registered owner if a pet has been chipped.

As for chipping humans, well that's not really necessary these days, although once they have all the pets chipped and we have all been predictively programmed to accept that they are safe to use on humans.

All of the infrastructure is in place to track and trace your every step without a microchip, and these days those mobile devices along with almost constant connection to the 'net' George Orwell was on the money. 2 and 2 makes five, Winston. Doubleplus good.

Even your 'smart' television can spy on you these days, along with your mobile telephone, Google is always listening and programs like Facebook also track what you do.

The fact that government spy agencies across the world have reciprocal arrangements with each other, enables them to share information.

Annie Machon, an ex British intelligence officer, highlighted the fact that because it was not permitted for domestic spy agencies to routinely snoop on their own populations, agencies would simply information share, after spying on each other's residents.

Nowadays there's probably no need to have such arrangements in place, since sweeping powers have been granted to such agencies to enable them to spy on whoever they like, under the guise of fighting the war on terror.

Micro managed society

The social architects that have worked with their surplus cash on the goal of micro managing society for generations, have apparently concluded that the only way to enact their goals is via a totalitarian dictatorship. There is no other way that their goals can be achieved.

Actually it seems to me that the 'would be' world managers aren't really that smart.

They spend enormous sums of money and put effort into controlling reproduction, yet at the same time they want to lower living standards to a low uniform level across the world.

Yet if they realised that the lower the living standards, the higher the birth rate, perhaps they would understand that if they raised the living standards across the world, then the birth rate would reduce all on its own.

Perhaps though, that they do know this, and they are simply such meanies that they don't want you living in a comfortable state.

As Aldous Huxley famously pointed out when interviewed by Mike Wallace back in the day, the agenda seeks to impose the dictatorship by consensus, with a willing populace who will enjoy their servitude, even in situations that they ought not to.

I think the words he actually used were 'people would love their servitude..'

And so now I understand it, I think.

The way that the agenda has rolled forwards to date includes a significant element of people who are willing minions of the globalist agenda.

The reason is because they think they are a part of the system, and therefore special.

I remember once being called to an emergency meeting at a local government, a few years back when they were worried about a flu pandemic.

This was a few years ahead of the 2009 swine flu outbreak.

Every department was in attendance, and the meeting was to identify which teams provided essential services, because in the event of a flu pandemic, there would only be limited availability of vaccines, and so they would make available the flu shots for those people involved in those teams deemed 'essential services.'

No doubt most of those present that had been determined to be essential service providers walked away from the meeting feeling special, that in the event of a pandemic they would be front of the queue for their vaccine.

I have also sat on disaster response teams, involving coordination with all local authorities which has included all sorts of scenario planning.

Agenda 21

I have previously scrutinised Agenda 21 and commented on it extensively.

I once gave a talk on it which took over an hour. I won't go into too much detail here.

The driving force of Agenda 21 - sustainable development, again brought to us via a branch of the United Nations.

Just about every human activity and bit of modern day infrastructure is classed as unsustainable, and if I had to describe Agenda 21 in less than 5 words it would be 'An incremental land seizure.' But there is a lot more to it than that.

So Agenda 21 put together back in 1992, was due for an update, which brings me to Agenda 2030.

Agenda 2030

As per before on the surface we have a noble series of goals, ending poverty and so on.

In their own words:

'we have adopted a historic decision on a comprehensive, far-reaching and people-centred set of universal and transformative Goals and targets.'

https://sustainabledevelopment.un.org/post2015/trans formingourworld

So, it's all about people, and the 'far-reaching' goals are going to be transformative.

This is of course big news and notable in its absence from the mainstream media, in anything other than supportive terms.

It would be remarkable to see this plan result in an end to poverty and hunger, but based on the U.N. track record I won't be surprised if they miss the target as per usual.

The evidence of the global micro management plan being a socialist dictatorship is indicated through the language used:

As we embark on this great collective journey, we pledge that no one will be left behind.

The collective wet dream.

In these Goals and targets, we are setting out a supremely ambitious and transformational vision.

Yes, in a nutshell, sustainable development to seize the land and sustainable medicine to control the units in their high density settlements.

Agenda 2030 seems to go beyond hopeful in all its visions.

'We envisage a world free of poverty, hunger, disease and want, where all life can thrive. We envisage a world free of fear and violence.'

It will be interesting to see how that is going to be achieved, based on the current state of worldwide geopolitical affairs.

Perhaps some of the methods will reveal themselves further into their blurb, we shall see..

There are 169 targets in Agenda 2030. Some examples include:

We commit to making fundamental changes in the way that our societies produce and consume goods and services

Perhaps their number 35 sums it up:

Sustainable development cannot be realized without peace and security.

Perhaps they should be in discussion with their cousins over at NATO who are busily building up troops near the Russian border.

To really get into the content, however it requires some reading on some of the action plans mentioned:

We support the implementation of relevant strategies and programmes of action, including the Istanbul Declaration and Programme of Action, the SIDS Accelerated Modalities of Action (SAMOA) Pathway, the Vienna Programme of Action for Landlocked Developing Countries for the Decade 2014-2024, and reaffirm the importance of supporting the African Union's Agenda 2063 and the programme of the New Partnership for Africa's Development (NEPAD), all of which are integral to the new Agenda.

Whilst Agenda 21 talked about the transfer of wealth and resources from developed nations to developing nations, Agenda 2030 seems to focus even more on those developing nations, whilst not mentioning the de-industrialisation of those developed countries.

Number 44 on the list is also interesting:

'We acknowledge the importance for international financial institutions to support, in line with their mandates, the policy space of each country..'

In other words they continue to support the imposition of IMF and World Bank loans along with conditionality clauses that will ensure the continued fire sale of assets in those nations.

Number 45 on the list confirms it is being pushed to local government level :

We acknowledge also the essential role of national parliaments through their enactment of legislation and adoption of budgets and their role in ensuring accountability for the effective implementation of our commitments. Governments and public institutions will also work closely on implementation with regional and local authorities..'

The SDGs and targets are integrated and indivisible, global in nature and universally applicable..

Of course a central component is action on climate change, which is another UN oxymoron as I will get to in the next chapter.

Climate change action

I think one of the reasons that there is so much confusion regarding climate change is because those that have looked at the issue realise that there are many environmental issues that are causing or have the potential to cause damage to our planet, but many people also believe that reducing carbon dioxide will address the 'biggest threat to mankind ever' global frigging warming.

The fact that people blindly believe that experts can limit any warming to less than 2 degrees Celsius by reducing carbon dioxide is ridiculous and will not address any of the real environmental problems going on in this world.

Oh so now I am a climate change denier.

I am not a climate change denier.

I acknowledge that the climate is changing, as it always has done.

However, my view is that since historically there have previously been numerous ice ages, we need climate adaptation strategies to guide us forwards, not ridiculous throttling of carbon dioxide attempts to limit any warming to 2 degrees Celcius.

There is no scientific proof that there is any impact on temperature difference between 350 ppm and 450 ppm.

None at all, even in a controlled environment, all elevated carbon dioxide does is produce improved plant growth.

Sure there are toxins, particulates in the air and contaminants in our ground water, but carbon dioxide reduction isn't going to fix any of those things.

One of the Sustainable Development goals is:

Goal 13. Take urgent action to combat climate change and its impacts

There are more than a few issues surrounding goal 13. Possibly one of the most dangerous parts of this goal are the range of suggested actions and actual interference in the atmosphere that have the potential to do untold damage to our entire ecosystem.

Imagine a bunch of crazy scientists given massive funding to concoct elaborate methods of deploying science into the ecosystem.

The range of 'solutions' has ranged from wonders like dumping iron into the ocean, to spraying reflective particles into the upper atmosphere to reflect sunlight.

Projects with fancy sounding names like solar radiation management and cloud seeding programs have included spraying all sorts of nasty particulates into the atmosphere.

Whilst such spraying programs have been laughed off by most folk as a whacky conspiracy theory, the people who are being funded to conduct such programs have openly discussed them.

Notably absent from discussions have been the potential negative impacts on human and other life underneath where the spraying programs have taken place.

If we are to get serious about minimising the human impact on the environment, the first thing that needs to be done is to ditch the demonization of carbon dioxide, and target specific real pollutants, in order of their toxicity and potential to damage flor and fauna. If a top 20 list were compiled, carbon dioxide wouldn't make the list.

Unfortunately however, since the IPCC driven ideology relies so heavily on hating carbon dioxide, woe betide anyone who dares question the validity of the so called settled science – which by the way is total bullshit.

Any time I hear the science is settled I know its bullshit.

The reason I mention both Agenda 21 and climate change is because so much money, time and effort are being directed towards them, and yet most folk are relatively uninformed about these things and yet they are significant influencers on development of strategies at most local governments today. That's another one, not believing the ideology of the carbon dioxide reduction cult will upset people too. Add it to the list.

The biggest threat to the climate comes from the climate manipulators, along with the people who have blind faith in the 'experts' because those folk will let those lunatics do anything to save them from the global warming bogeyman.

Government 'shut the f up program'

When I worked for another level of government, I was sent to an information session titled ethical decision making or something like that.

It's quite a common thing to attend these type of information sessions, the purpose is to avoid any conflicts of interest when working for governments.

This one particular information session went a bit further than that.

The presenter was basically saying that you shouldn't say anything about anyone at any level of government.

I got into an argument with someone over it, making the point that it's a free country and I don't get paid for my own spare time, and whilst I understood the concept of not expressing an opinion in the capacity as a representative of the organisation, but would, as an individual have an opinion and a right to express that opinion if I so chose to do and that was my business.

The person I was arguing with seemed to think it was not ok to say anything of a political nature.

So I renamed it the 'shut the f up program.

It was quite funny at the time, though, since I was and had been quite politically active in communicating with

MP's and so on regarding various issues, like telling Wayne Swan 'told you so' regarding the national finances.

When I, along with many other people communicated concerns about the proposed Carbon tax, Malcolm Turnbull cracked the shits and complained to the local media that people had tried to 'blow up' his party, because the massive fight it caused within its ranks between those who saw the scam for what it was and those that continued to push the idea.

The Corporation

I had been trained for 5 years with my own team of over 50 staff by a giant corporation that had been in business for 100 years, so I got a good base in team management.

The Corporation was in the majority of countries around the world and the division I worked for was just one of several, with about 300,000 employees.

They had an entire section working on R&D and so I got to learn best practice within my chosen field.

Over the next few years I got to manage a variety of teams and in general management, got to learn about budgeting, business planning and performance management in greater detail.

Then I realised that to make further progress in my career I should get some qualifications, so I got them.

Having had a mixture of private sector and local government I also have a reasonable handle on the differences between the two.

I will also say that even though the private sector will claim until the cows come home that they are the specialists and should leave it to them to do whatever it is, rather than a local government, but in my experience that isn't true, local governments are able to do a comparable job in just about anything that the private sector can, particularly when one considers the fact that a council can provide its own service in-house at cost, whereas a contractor will generally be cost plus profit.

It all comes down to the people who work there and the processes in place.

Journey into Local Government

My foray into local government started out as a bit of a nightmare, even if it sounded good on paper.

The new job paid more money than I was getting in the previous job I had, the role as Operations Manager required me to drive to work in my own Audi 200 turbo.

In the job before that in the private sector I had a Renault Clio as a company car, so that made a pleasant change.

It all sounded good, a great new challenge for me. The job had higher wages, and a step up the ladder from a supervisor to a manager.

After one week into the job, I picked up the telephone and called my previous employer in the private sector and asked them if I could come back.

I couldn't believe how much power there was in the hands of the workers in a highly unionised environment, and because I had been given the brief to run the place like I would have in my previous job in the private sector, I quickly realised that the two were incompatible, and at the time I didn't have the skills or experience to manage it.

I was handed a handful of overtime claim forms from staff by the administration officer.

I refused to sign the forms, and said that if they were to be authorised then a justification would have to be provided, and that 'lots of work' wasn't a valid justification unless accompanied by further explanation, for example, truck broken down for 2 hours, 2 hours overtime.

The Union rep came to my desk to lean on me and make me sign the forms, a big bear of a man in a gorilla-like stance, leaning over my desk with the knuckles on his paws burying into the desk in front of me, and then barked

"You gonna sign these forms or what?"

I told him I was not going to sign them unless accompanied by the justification.

He spun around and marched off shaking his head, headed towards the muster room, presumably to tell the guys the outcome.

 The supervisor stormed into the office, and threw his keys across the desk at me and said "get another supervisor then."

I still said no.

The Director who had overheard the 'fracas' instructed me to pay it.

I walked in to the muster room to let the team know that they would be getting all overtime claimed.

As I walked out of there, I felt a bit silly. That's when I picked up the telephone and called my old boss, and went straight back in to the private sector.

Local Governments that believe in the snake oil salesman

Some of the biggest scammers are hailed as gurus in many local governments. Al 'it's inconvenient that the hockey stick is baloney, and we added footage from a fictional movie to make you believe the inconvenient truth' Gore is one of them.

Al came to Australia, and trained a load of people in what to say, when giving lectures to people on climate change. People volunteered for the 'project climate connect' which was in my opinion rolled out like a bunch of missionaries might have back in the old colonial days when spreading the word through previously unchartered territories.

The 'project connect' group was something that I signed up to, since at the time I believed in all that nonsense about reducing carbon dioxide and global warming.

Actually it was the paperwork that the climate connect gang sent me that made me look a bit closer. It looked a bit like a swastika.

Anyway, fast forward a bit and I found out all the errors of the movie that Al also got an Oscar for, and then that he stood to profiteer from the implementation of the carbon trading game.

Also, whilst all the local government believers in Al Gore got really shitty with me for pointing out the hypocrisy of some self-proclaimed global warming guru, I carried on with the questions.

Why was it ok for some bloke with a mansion that used more electricity than 20 houses, to lecture me about being more environmentally aware to the point of demanding that I be taxed for it?

Didn't he also own an aircraft and a boat?

And whilst telling everyone fictional tales about massive sea level rises, he purchased property on the coast?

Actually, I seem to recall the local global warming guru, space commander Flannery also purchased waterside property.

Space commander Flannery, you know that model Australian who wants us all to be like ants in a colony and only permitted to perform certain tasks, like breeding.

The main differences between local government and the private sector

The differences between a job in local government and the private sector depend on what level the job being compared is at.

Rostered days off, leaving loading, 38 hour weeks are all concepts largely alien to workers in the private sector, but are quite common employment conditions in local government.

At higher levels, managers and executives can probably get more money in the private sector for most job types, but whilst they may also benefit from not having to attend Council Meetings, typically management do have a bit of travelling to do for regular meetings regardless of whether they are in the private sector or local government.

Overall, in my experience, the number of meetings attended in local government surpasses anything I have seen in the private sector – by a country mile.

On top of the regular team meetings, there's committee meetings, briefing meetings, focus groups, working groups, information sessions, and so on in local governments.

I suppose on one level it's not fair to make a comparison between the two, since they are vastly different in nature and have different goals.

However, I will make the point that I have been 'roped in' to many a meeting that I have had little contribution to make and have often been at a meeting and thought to myself about other more pressing demands on my time, and wondered how many other people at the meeting felt the same.

One Glaring Omission

Elected representatives within local government, and officers for that matter, often have to declare if they have a financial or other interest in any matter being considered.

Whilst this is all transparent, the one big omission is that council officials don't also have to declare any other outside interests or affiliations.

Shouldn't we know if that elected person has pledged allegiance to anything else?

The Banished Manager and Jackie Sackem

So after my first nightmarish work experience working for a municipality, the next time the opportunity came to work for a local government, I was quite apprehensive, especially as it was for a local government on the other side of the world.

In Australia, I worked for a local government where the workforce took such offence to how their manager spoke to them, that they had a vote of no confidence in him, and took industrial action by picketing the front gate at the depot.

The manager was banished from the depot that he was in charge of and was relocated to a part of the Town Hall which was unused – the original Council chambers.

I went to visit him and found him sitting at the head of an enormous table, the room lined with framed portraits of previous elected Mayors.

He told me that part of the conditions he had been given were that he was also forbidden to talk to any of the 50 or so of his staff, and that any communications would have to go through via a supervisor.

Actually he was also a good mentor for me and at least he worked hard.

I think the problem was a lot of people misunderstood him, but he was always good to me and at least he wasn't one of those handballing types, you know the ones, that wear the Teflon pants, every bit of work that comes their way slides off them and delegated to everyone else.

When the manager eventually left, a member of the management team who had been brought in to act in the manager's role, approached me and 'strongly suggested' that I should put in an application for the vacant manager position.

Obviously I was spurred on with enthusiasm, especially as management were encouraging me to put in an application.

I put in my application for the position and waited to be called for an interview.

A couple of weeks later, whilst sitting at my desk in my office, I was introduced to my new manager.

I was shocked.

I asked the acting manager later on that day what had happened as I didn't even get an interview, after being encouraged to apply.

'Yeah that was a bit poor not to get back to you'.

Go figure.

Anyway the new manager was nicknamed variously the toe cutter and Jackie Sack-em.

One time I was filling in for the building maintenance supervisor who was away on leave.

Since he was on long service leave, I also had his vehicle, and being that building maintenance issues could happen at any time, whilst acting in the role I had full unlimited use of it.

I was at home and heard a bang at the door. There was a note on the fly screen door.

Scribbled on the piece of paper was a note from Jackie Sackem.

It said 'URGENT CALL ME NOW'.

I called his mobile number.

He was mightily displeased, I could tell as he was screaming at me over the phone.

He demanded for me to bring the building maintenance supervisor car over to him at the tennis club, which was about a twenty minute drive from my home, in order to save him the embarrassment of being at the jolly old tennis club in a workman's utility vehicle.

I told him I was eating dinner and the answer was "no".

He repeated his demand in an even more enraged tone.

I repeated it back to him "so let me get this right you want me to drop what I am doing, drive over to your tennis club and swap vehicles with you?"

I told him the chances of that happening were zero, goodbye, and hung up the phone.

The next day he called me in to the office and told me he was going to give me a written warning for using the vehicle for private use and I only had commuting use rights.

I tried to point out that I was acting in the BM role which had private use, but he just had to show me. How dare I put him in the position of only having a utility vehicle to show up for the tennis in!

The hypocrisy wasn't apparent at the time.

He was lecturing me about appropriate use of resources, but in fact, as I later found out, he had cashed in his entitlement to use of a council vehicle, and was paid additional cash to use his own car.

He shouldn't have been driving any Council vehicle.

I left soon after that.

After I left, I heard that the old manager had left the council, after one of the supervisors that reported to him died of a heart attack.

The guys largely blamed Jackie sakem for this, saying that he drove him into the ground by putting too much pressure on him.

My next time in a local government was about 1 year later, as I had scrambled back to the private sector for a while.

Silly me, I returned to local government.

Actually the next one was ok, but the next few after that were not ok.

The following are some more of the highlights from my time employed in local government.

The incompetent manager

Incompetent managers aren't exclusively found in local governments, but I have certainly encountered more than a few in my time working at various Councils.

A colleague of mine once gave me his explanation for the phenomenon of incompetence from management.

"Incompetent managers surround themselves with others who are more incompetent than they are, to make themselves look relatively good. That's why, if you are good at what you do, watch out you might find yourself under fire. If you want to make it in local government, keep your head down and don't do anything to draw attention to yourself."

Another colleague gave me his explanation for it.

"The further up the hierarchy you look, the greater the level of incompetence."

More recently, another colleague summed it up by saying

"No good deed goes unpunished in local government."

In the early days I thought that these individuals were wrong, that what they were referring to were isolated cases, the exception rather than the rule.

However, after more than 20 years in the game I am not convinced that these are isolated situations, and that incompetent management is possibly more widespread than we realise, whether it is in the private sector or local government.

In local government one of the reasons for this might be because they tend to place a high value on qualifications alone.

For example, I once applied for a job that I was shortlisted by a recruitment agency for, out of 80 applicants I was in the top 3, due to my extensive relevant experience.

I failed to get an interview because the recruiting Council wanted someone with a degree. Even the recruitment agent tried to argue my case, but the Council in their infinite wisdom were adamant that they wanted someone with a degree, not in any particular field.

It didn't matter what the degree was in, even if it was one that was totally unrelated to the job.

So potentially the job could have gone to someone with limited or no experience but because they had an art degree they could have the job.

Some of the bad managers I have encountered in local governments have included all sorts of unreasonable demands such as calling me at home when on annual leave to ask me to come back to work early, I have had to 'jump through hoops' over and above what is required in the documented policies for things like taking rostered days off and booking annual leave and it all seems to boil down to the fact that there are more than a few petty minded power trippers in management positions in local government, people who have unremarkable skills who seem content to hinder the productive efforts of others by exerting their power to justify their existence.

Presumably some of those managers never got the memo, that the old top-down dictatorial model of yesteryear has been surpassed.

Good management these days is all about enabling staff to achieve their goals, to empower and assist with ensuring that teams have the support and resources required to do the job.

Good management will ensure a happy productive workforce, compared to bad management which only sets the stage for unhappy and unproductive workers.

Ranger Wars

I don't know why they call them Rangers they generally would be more aptly called 'dog catchers' because in my experience that seems to be about all the Rangers I have met do.

I have met some exceptions - good people who are Rangers but I have also met some absolute scum bags, presumably attracted to the position because they get a badge and the ability to dish out fines.

I remember overhearing a couple of them once joking about how they would see how far a dog would get once the 'green juice' had been administered before they dropped dead.

Once a dog has been in the pound for a while if it's not re-homed then they put them down. In some cases they just throw the dead bodies into a bin.

I was horrified to find out that under the relevant Act, they are only required to keep a dog for 72 hours before killing it, although in most cases they do keep them in the pound for a couple of weeks.

I put their jokes down to the fact that it must be an awful job, being there whilst perfectly healthy dogs are exterminated, and that it was just their way of dealing with what would be a difficult part of their job.

Anyway the reason I mentioned the Rangers was that I got into a big fight with them. (Well not all of them, but some of them.)

It may have been that I was on their radar because my dog used to jump the fence and go wandering through the suburb which was right next to where I worked.

I used to get the heads up when someone called in that there was a dog roaming and/or chasing cats in the neighbourhood.

Anyway I always used to get the jump on the call and find my dog before the Rangers got there.

One day they had taken a call and picked up a young dog that was sitting at the roadside next to another which had been hit by a car.

This dog was due to be put down as no-one took it, so I suggested my neighbour take the dog.

I already had my hands full with my rescued from death row dog.

So the neighbour took the dog, and had him for a few weeks until one day was taken back to the pound for the offence of running in a park off the lead in an area not allowed.

The neighbour didn't have the money to get the dog back out of the pound, normally in such a situation, particularly as it was a young dog, it would have been advertised in the local paper as dog of the week in an attempt to rehome the dog.

Instead, one of the Rangers that had taken a dislike to me, came into my office specifically to tell me that they weren't going to be advertising the dog and they were going to have it put down instead.

I was outraged and went to the rangers office to argue for the dogs life. One of the Rangers put his hands up and proclaimed that it wasn't his decision.

I called the Rangers' boss, who was at the main administration building and asked him to come and see the dog for himself. He refused, presumably couldn't be bothered.

I went fucking nuts, I got on the email system, and I emailed every single fucker in that organisation, every elected council member, the Mayor, the CEO, you name it I copied them all in, to try and stop those fucks from killing that dog.

I had one single email in support, with a solitary phone call from one elected councillor who expressed any concern.

The rest of the day, my fucking phone rang off the hook with outraged wankers who were demanding my apologies be given to the head ranger and withdrawal of my emails and so on.

Absolutely bonkers!

Roundup questions

Of all the local governments I have worked for, only one of them decided to ditch Roundup and try something more environmentally friendly.

Just in case you didn't know, Roundup is the most common name for Glyphosate which is one of the most commonly used chemicals that are sprayed across municipalities across the world, primarily to control weeds.

One Council I worked for that decided to try an alternative, used steam – water. The main problem with this is that it typically costs up to thrice as much.

It absolutely shits me that so many blinkered people keep on believing in the marketing of this product and laugh at the silly folk who dare to question the safety of the product.

Is it safe?

No. I once worked for a local government and the Safety Advisor told me that a worker had once died as a result of accidentally swallowing Roundup when he tried to manually siphon some from one container to another.

Also, anyone who has ever seen their local council workers spraying parks and other public open spaces will probably have also seen the placement of warning signage whilst the spraying is being done.

As soon as they have finished, however, the warning signs are taken away and potentially, dog walkers and people walking through with their children immediately behind the workers may walk through oblivious to the fact that the area has just been sprayed.

Many nations have now banned Glyphosate, and the corporate whore media continues on saying that all the concerns are based on 'junk science.'

[52]

When the W.H.O. stated that it was 'probably carcinogenic' in 2015, and presumably following some persuasion by Monsanto, in 2016 the conclusion was revised to say that it probably wasn't a carcinogenic "risk to humans from exposure through the diet."

Of course, Roundup is a significant component in the Monsanto arsenal, since they have developed 'Roundup Ready' GMO crops which are resistant to Roundup whilst killing weeds.

One Norwegian University looked at GM Soy products and concluded

That compared to Monsanto's own guidance, 5.6 milligrams of Roundup per kilogram of plant weight would be considered extreme.

The Norwegian researchers found an average of 9 milligrams of Roundup per kilogram. [51]

Again this is downplayed, with the defenders sending out their minions to dispel any concerns about the widespread spraying, saying that they don't really spray that much. Hello?

The regional 'open cheque book' project

I am going to go into some considerable detail with the following chapter, not least because I kept my own personal diary.

Imagine if you will, a regional project which involved a group of local governments, jointly working through a regional group to achieve a common goal.

A noble cause!

I worked for the regional group at its start up so had a fairly good understanding of what the project involved and where things were at.

This project was notable in a few regards, but particularly the agreement between the group of Councils, which was effectively an open cheque book for the regional organisation that was established to manage the project.

The clause in the agreement which allowed for 'open slather' was one which stated that each member council would pay their share of the costs incurred, without limitation.

This particular project required a loan of tens of millions of dollars.

One might be forgiven for thinking that such a project would have resulted in significant scrutiny from the member councils.

However the regional group were set up in such a manner that it was very difficult to attempt to raise any awkward questions. I wonder how many other regional local governments have similar issues.

As I have seen many times, frequently large infrastructure projects get bogged down in contractual legalities. In the one I was involved in, that included being offered technical specifications that were outside the scope of what had been tendered.

Despite this, they got what was offered by the supplier instead.

The regional group was set up like a council in its own right, with a Chairman and elected members, which consisted of councillors from the member councils.

There was also a regional executive group which consisted of senior management from the member councils.

The problem was that most of the senior executive members, the representatives from each council didn't have operational experience in the project on a daily basis.

I did, and so I would regularly scan through the meeting agenda notes and prepared a detailed list of questions for my own executive representative to ask on behalf of the council I worked for at the regional executive meetings.

I wasn't allowed to attend as I was just a mere manager.

The CEO of the regional group became infuriated with me personally presumably for asking too many questions, and made it his mission to discredit me to my director.

I put up with that CEO's attacks for about 5 years.

From my perspective, all I was doing was holding the regional group to account properly and transparently and representing the interests of the ratepayers in the council I worked for.

When the project was still at conceptual stage, it was sold to the member councils as being so good that one day, the project would begin to generate revenue for the member councils, rather than increase costs.

However, once the project became operational, it became clear that this would never happen.

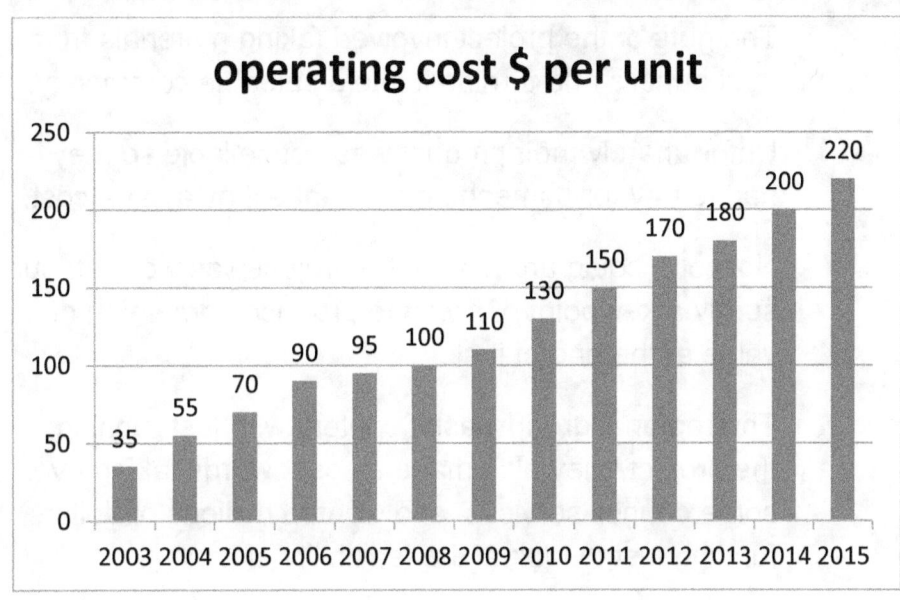

operating cost $ per unit

Figure 1: Costs per unit of the project (approximate) 2003-2015

The difference in cost per unit might not sound that much, rising steadily from around $35 per unit in 2003 up to $220 in 2015, but remembering that there were multiple councils in on the project and in some councils the total number of units over the year were up to tens of thousands, it had a significant impact on the budget and hence the ratepayer.

It also highlights the vast difference between what it was sold as and what it actually delivered.

Outrageous you say? Why didn't anyone hold their feet to the fire on this?

Well, I did, or at least I tried my best to.

The guts of the project involved taking materials from the councils and turning it into a saleable commodity.

Unfortunately their product was not sellable so they had to pay for someone else to take it away at a cost.

Now one could argue that the project was worth it, but surely a key point of it was to produce something of value at the end of it all.

The regional group wasn't content with just running the project, they also made steps towards taking over some council services, and wanted millions of dollars funding just to look at the feasibility of it all.

I helped stop that from happening and I would like to think I helped hold their feet to the flame as much as I could.

It started out with me being given some of the regional group's strategic and operational documents to review and comment on.

I put forward the argument that the regional group were tasked with getting the project operating as it should have been, rather than expanding their empire through diversification, to be achieved by taking over services already provided by the member councils.

My boss agreed, and their proposed 2 million dollars to establish the feasibility and plan to take over those services was stopped in its tracks.

The following is an example of my input into some of the strategic planning matters a couple of years into the project.

It really started when I began trawling through the strategic documents.

There were some nebulous budget proposals. Initially I did this from about 2004 and on an ongoing basis.

In one of the activities, they proposed a 2.5 million dollar. I asked them what this was actually to be used for, as the performance indicators were inadequate as there was only a cost effectiveness measure and nothing about quality.

The next item they had budgeted for another 3.5 million dollars in 2005 with again no quality of service indicators.

The next item related to processing costs.

It just so happened that I had all the information required to work out their cost per tonne and total tonnes should be the total budget required for this, and in this case the total should have been less than 400,000.

However this had a proposed budget of $702,000.

It wasn't overhead costs, as they were paid separately.

The next item I came to was an 80 percent increase in Capital Expenditure compared to the 2001 figure.

This was a new facility just up and running for a couple of years, and all plant and equipment should last for at least 5 years.

I just asked the question as to what the cause of this extra expense was for.

There was also a budgeted $75000 for the sale of a major asset without any further detail.

I suspected it was a piece of processing equipment which had failed to live up to expectations, but I asked the question anyway.

I was sure by then that I was being a total pain in the arse in asking so many questions, but I considered it a part of my role and would have been inappropriate not to.

It was obvious by 2005 that there were going to be ongoing emissions issues relating to the processing, and it all started to become more serious towards the end of 2005, with vocal action groups regularly taking their stories to the local media.

It was difficult to get information regarding what measures were being taken to address the problem.

I put my ear close to the ground and from what I could determine, the cause of the odours was due to either a lack of maintenance and/or poor design of filtration units.

Also the fact that they were also processing really smelly shit may have had something to do with it.

They said that they would stop accepting the really smelly shit, but that didn't address the filtration issues, and they hadn't put forward any budget proposals to implement any significant improvements or take any steps towards fixing the problem.

I actually said something like : ' This is an issue that potentially could escalate to the point of the facility getting closed down or cause significant negative publicity.'

By March 2006 I pushed as hard as I could to alert senior management that the odour problem required urgent remedial action.

I followed this up with several more emails on the subject that still nothing was being done to sort the problem out.

I predicted that the site would be closed pending remedial action, but I didn't say 'told you so' at the time, when it did get closed down for a period of months - perhaps I should have.

The facility did eventually re-open after they implemented the required remedial action.

At least the project wasn't as bad as what happened in Victoria, with an estimated $60 million dollars spent on an IT project which was subsequently ditched by the Department of Justice. [50]

Over in the UK, the New Statesman reported on a range of costly Council projects involving disputes and cost blow outs. [49]

Compaction woes

For a few years, the issue of optimum density of the transported materials was a topic of discussion.

From a transportation perspective, the ideal density would coincide with the legal payload of the truck.

By restricting the density of the materials, it effectively reduced each load delivered for processing, from 5 tonnes to 4 tonnes.

With each truck doing at least 2 runs per day, and multiple trucks in each council, the net effect was a requirement for additional trucks.

I put up the case to move from 25 M3 trucks, to 29 M3 tucks, to offset the reduced compaction.

The council I worked for required about an additional 0.6 trucks with the compaction limitation.

A neighbouring Council were going to tender which required 1.5 trucks, so by putting in a tender for the other Council and a business case for 2 additional trucks meant that both could be serviced at industry best rates.

The day we won the contract to collect and transport the other councils material, the regional group CEO proudly announced he was going to implement a financial penalty against any load delivered to more than the agreed density.

My team started researching to see whether there had been much research done in the area of density and compaction levels of transported materials, to find out what the industry best practice was.

I knew that the optimum density from a purely transportation perspective was the legal load limit, but with the other considerations, I wasn't completely sure, although I did know that visually anyone would have difficulty in identifying which load was which, if for instance you placed one load at 180 kg/M and the other at 200.

It turned out that there wasn't much information available, but from the work that had been done, the results were far from conclusive, but did suggest that excessive compaction limitations could impact on operating costs by up to 25 percent, but at compaction levels of more than 220kg per M3 the damage to the materials started to become significant.

The compaction limit we were constrained to was 150 kg per M.

The trucks could legally carry at around 200 kg per M3.

We were making the case for the compaction level to be a more reasonable 180 kg per M3, being the balance between operational efficiency without significantly impacting on the materials being transported.

A discussion paper on the subject was tabled for inclusion at the Regional Executive meeting.

It was rejected.

Then the regional group showed my director a draft of a 'operational efficiency' report targeting my team.

In essence, the report was trying to say that I was running the truck fleet inefficiently and if that was fixed then compaction wouldn't be a problem.

The evidence they provided included analysis of each truck load that had been delivered to the facility.

They were trying to say, here, look this truck load was only half full, you could have made better use of it. You have a load here that wasn't full.

So I went over the figures.

Unfortunately they had made some wrong assumptions which amount to significant errors, which included making the assumption that all the trucks were the same capacity.

They were not. In fact the largest truck had more than double the capacity as the smallest.

When the correct truck data was put into their own charts, the conclusion put the operational effectiveness level was over 95% which was in line with industry best practice.

So, knowing that they intended to table that report to the Regional Executive, I put up our corrected version.

They pulled their report from the agenda.

Acceptance woes

So, there I was, managing the largest team of all the other participant Councils in this project, for which I had special permission to sign off on the loan repayment for the Capital costs, which were a few hundred thousand dollars per quarter just for this one Council alone.

The project was up and running.

Then someone called to say take your material somewhere else.

That brand new facility was closed.

We actually had a Mexican stand-off at the regional facility.

I had a couple of trucks that I had told to go there as usual.

Whilst en route, I called the regional group to tell them that the trucks were coming, you better let them in.

They pleaded with me not to send the trucks, but my view was that it was their job to take the material and their problem if a piece of machinery was broken down, they should have some contingency plans in place. I repeated this view at the management group meeting, which was met with a shrug of shoulders and no response.

When the trucks arrived on the weighbridge, I received a call from a distressed truck driver, who informed me that the bloke at the facility entrance was threatening to call the police.

I said to the driver what on earth are they going to say?

Hello this is the regional council, one of our member councils won't leave the site that they part own, evidenced by the logo on the building?

In the absence of a solution, I came up with a plan to ensure the material wasn't just disposed of like the regional group suggested we did.

We found an area near a golf course that was suitable for making a holding pen for the material. The problem was that it had to be double handled, but at least the material wasn't wasted, as we simply stored it until the facility was ready to receive us again.

The dramas with the facility being out of action happened a few times, but the thing that realy pissed me off was when the regional group decided that every time we delivered the materials to another alternative site, we would still have the pay the regional group the regional rate, and they would pick up the tab from the alternative facilities.

The problem with this was that the other facilities were half the cost, and in effect by allowing this would perhaps give the regional group an incentive to not be open for business.

The end of year budget was summarised.

The operating expenses, at just over 6 million dollars in the budget had blown out to 7.1 million. Income was about 500,000 dollars below expectations giving a 1.4 million dollar blow out on a 6 million dollar budget.

This resulted in a jump of 35 percent in the processing costs for the next financial year.

More alarmingly was that the facility was accepting commercial entries.

The figures appeared to show that the costs to process were about $5 per tonne more than they were receiving from commercial entries.

The figures showed an operating loss of 2.4 million for the following 2 years.

The budget allowed for up to 45 percent of the material processed to be disposed of as waste after processing, but the actual was showing over 54 percent.

The facility reported having staff employed directly, but closer scrutiny revealed that 6 out of the 22 staff – 27 percent – were listed as labour hire casuals.

Also, despite the implementation of the compaction limitations which was supposed to reduce waste material being disposed of, over 31 percent of the recyclable material was still going to waste.

The dramas went on and on and on.

The CEO left the organisation and then they appointed the replacement person without advertising the position which I thought was not in keeping with the requirements of the Local Government Act but I wasn't sure if there was some loophole that they had used so I didn't pursue that, even though I would have liked the opportunity to have put in for it.

I did go for a position at another regional council, and was interestingly also asked by a recruitment consultant who I thought my supporters had been at Council xyz. By the look on her face I guessed that she must have called someone at xyz council.

Sub prime slackers

Now I am no Warren Buffett, but if I had been in charge of investments at this particular council, they never would have gotten into such a situation where tens of millions of dollars were put at risk.

One might think it reasonable to assume that a council would only invest in low risk moderate return sort of things.

Actually that's not the case, for anyone who knows what happened in Orange County with their investments.

If you had 50 million, perhaps it would be split into cash, property and shares, or even cash property shares and commodities.

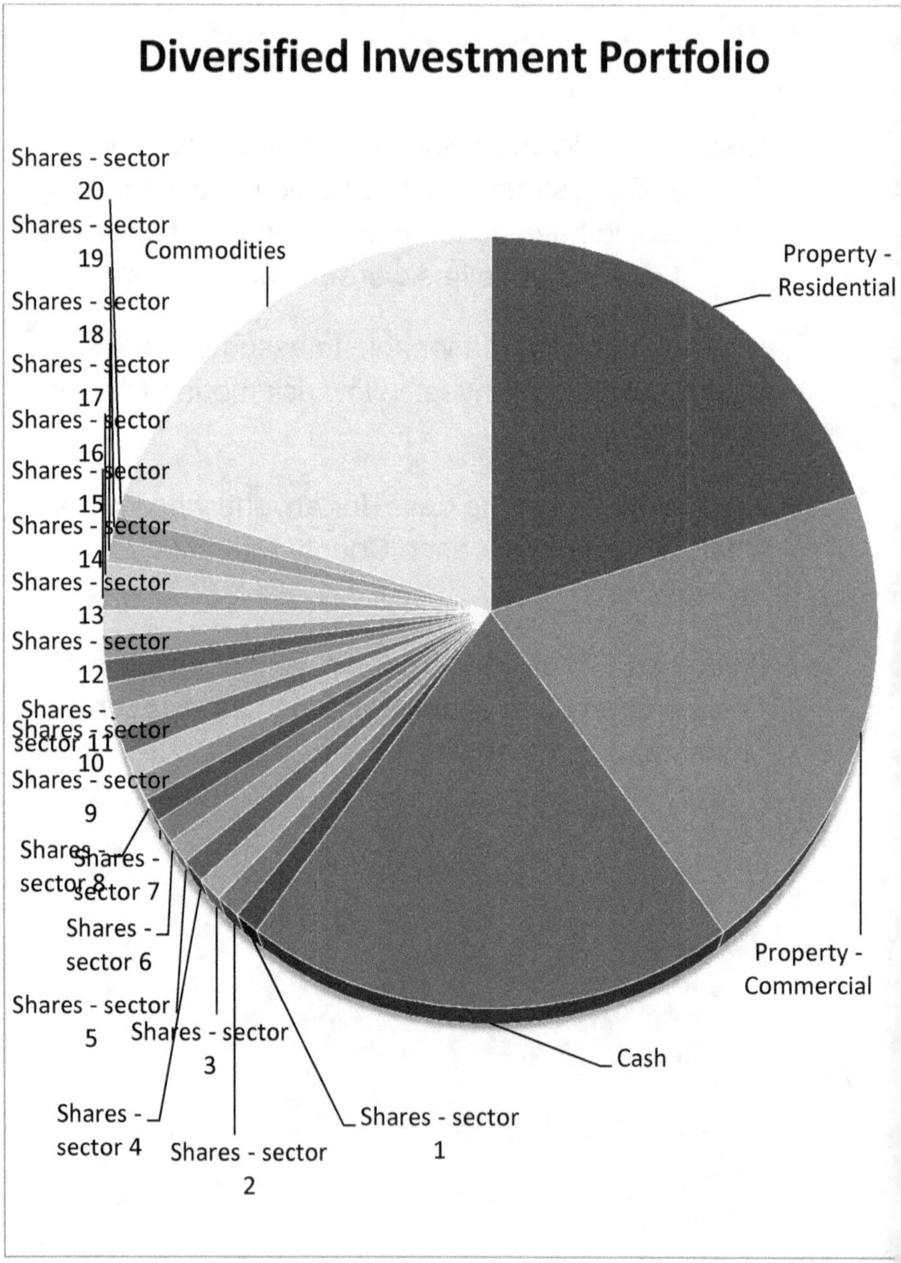

Diversified Investment Portfolio

Figure 2 : Ideally, 50 million dollars invested into a diversified portfolio including shares, cash, property and commodities would be split similarly to the above pie chart

So with say ten million dollars in shares, that would be further spread across all the sectors, and there are over 20 of them, so ball park figure would be 500,000 in any one sector, assuming you wanted to have a diverse investment portfolio.

But what did this one council do with their 50 million dollars invested? 20 million into sub prime Collateralised Debt Obligations – CDOs.

They had to fight to get it back but at one point it looked like they were going to lose it all.

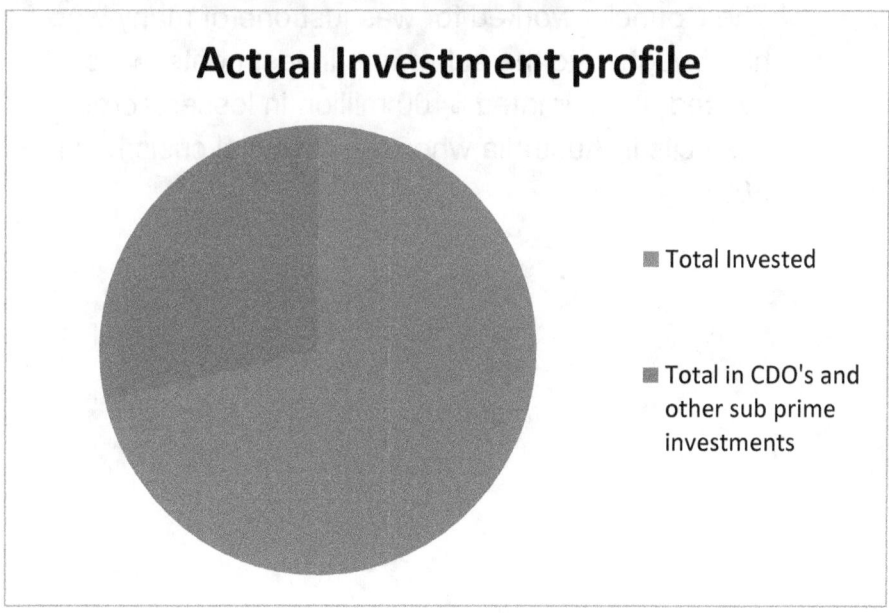

Figure 3 Out of approximately 50,000,000 dollars invested, around 20 million of it was invested in CDO and other high risk investments

The root causes of how approximately 40 percent of the total invested went into high risk investments included the fact that the investments had been sold, erroneously as AAA rated investments, and that the Council that invested in them had taken the investment advice on the basis that it was from an Advisor that was endorsed by the local government association. Presumably this was why no-one thought to check how the investment was going to provide the returns touted by the ivestment advisors. When it all turned to crap, the investment advisor disappeared.

The Council I worked for was just one of many who had bought into the sub-prime investments, which caused an estimated $400 million in losses across Councils in Australia when the financial crisis hit in 2008. [48]

Finance rogue

I worked for one local government where the newly appointed finance manager was hauled away by the cops, apparently he had embezzled a bit of cash from a previous local government he worked for, and it wasn't until he had moved jobs that the cops caught up with him.

At another Council I missed out on meeting one particular director who had taken it upon himself to supplement his generous salary package by stealing sandwiches from the catering team. He had been given the boot before I got there.

In 2016 the Finance Manager at Yorke Council in South Australia was charged with 60 counts of theft [47]

Over in the UK the same year, Newcastle City Council sacked a worker for falsely billing for over 12 million pounds [46]

You've got mail

Ok so we have all heard stories about how someone gets hauled over the coals for looking at porn at work, but what about the story about the bloke who got keel hauled for being the recipient of an x rated email?

Yes it was me, I received an email. The reason I received it was because I overheard the bloke who opened it shout out 'that's disgusting!'

I foolishly asked what was disgusting, and so he said ' I will send it to you.'

I knew those fuckers were snooping on my computer anyway and had left them some nice trails to follow.

My faux pas was apparently in not adhering to the IT Policy. According to the Policy, anyone who received an inappropriate email was required to forward it on to their manager, which I failed to do.

The irony that the hypocrites missed, was that in pulling me in to an impromptu disciplinary meeting without notice failed to comply with their own Human Resource Policy.

The fact that I had developed a replacement plan for assets to ensure that those assets were kept in accordance with the Policy, was neither here nor there when it came to budget time, I was given less than half the required budget. So much for sticking to the Policy, I thought.

I had reported something much more serious than that only a short time before, an incident in which I got stuck in to an administration officer who had returned a letter I had asked to be typed up and sent out, by placing it in the bottom of my intray. When I eventually found it, I discovered that it hadn't been sent out and approached the officer to point out that the bottom of my intray wasn't the place for the letter to be sent.

In response this person went into a rage, started crying and kicked a hole in the wall on the way out the door.

What did these zealous enforcers of the policy do about that? Well nothing that I know of.

It once again shows that over zealous power trippers can and will use technology to carry out all sorts of mischief. I should know, I participated in such a thing once on a member of staff that was claiming lots of overtime, it was suggested to me that I should verify it with the camera footage from the security video to check the hours worked matched those claimed.

At the time I didn't give it a moments' thought, but later realised that I was becoming a new world order minion.

Micro management via use of surveillance cameras, GPS and so on is on the rise, and more of this insanity is in the pipeline.

The concept of privacy is to be a thing of the past in the future.

Grudge holders incorporated

So when you tread on the wrong toes, sometimes it comes back to bite you on the arse.

A local Mayor once gave a great speech, which pointed out that one can have all the experience and qualifications in the world, but if one failed to work on having great working relations, or worse if one had bad working relationships then this was a recipe for disaster.

It was only then that I really became more considerate of diplomacy and tactfulness.

However, as I discovered, some folk will do their utmost to ruin your day, and they just don't let it go – ever!

I once called up a Council and wanted an explanation as to why I hadn't even got an interview. When I eventually went through from HR to the Director, the very first words out of his mouth, without prompting was "It wasn't like anyone put the boots in and said steer clear of that guy." I thought to myself that was strange, until I found out a previous boss had been meeting with management at that other Council.

I got some contracting work on another occasion, and went back to a previous Council where I had rattled some cages and discovered that they almost rejected the quote as soon as they saw my name on it, until someone else pointed out that it met their requirements and was the only quote.

So I had to sit there in a meeting with these grudge holding fuckers, knowing full well that they still had it in for me.

They must be really scared of me, or maybe scared of what I might say.

Who knows, but the point is we can all only do our best to have great working relationships and sometimes it doesn't matter what you do.

To my haters

A special message to my select band of haters, please realise that when you treat me badly it doesn't inspire me to be nice to you in return.

But thanks for reading my book. LOL.

Also keep in mind that I have notes of facts and figures to substantiate just about everything I have said in this book, so if anyone wants to make an issue out of anything I have said here, just remember that much of it falls into the realm of 'public interest' and if I have to give more detail to substantiate what I have said then I will gladly do so.

Yes all the haters out there should go and take a look in the mirror and see the hypocrisy of the petty bullshit and get some humanity!

I'm not generally one to blame others for my failings, having authored 3 books that failed to sell, having applied and been an also ran with countless job applications, having to effectively beg to borrow money from my parents in my 40's, and so on, I know all about failure and the importance of being able to pick yourself up out of the gutter and put one foot in front of the other.

The old Samurai saying 'fall down six times stand up 7.'

I do however believe that there is enough weight of evidence to support the notion that interference from some previous toes that I previously either deliberately or inadvertently stepped on have been a significant factor, but that brings me to the point about the fact that there is nothing we can do about what others think of us, and we shouldn't be so concerned about it because if they hate you that much, there isn't much chance of that changing anytime soon – especially if they are world record grudge holders.

I am reminded that whatever they think they know about you it might or might not be true yesterday but not necessarily today.

Don't throw more fuel on the fire by reinforcing it by what you do today. It's today and tomorrow that really counts, and as long as we do our best, sometimes that's all you can do.

Council workers sacked

I know there is a widespread perception, even amongst Council workers, that it's not common for full time staff to have their employment terminated for misconduct, unless it's something really serious such as theft or violence in the workplace.

However, this isn't quite true.

In 2014, two Gold Coast workers were fired for taking a break at the wrong time, which was reported by the media with the headline 'Council workers sacked for taking smoko at Surfers Paradise pie shop.' [45]

In 2009, two Geelong Council workers, one of them a long term employee, were sacked after they filled in a pothole at the place where they went for lunch, because they accepted a free sandwich afterwards. [44]

The workers were eventually reinstated.

In 2015, a 78 year old Tasmanian council worker with a mind boggling 62 years of service claimed age discrimination was behind his sacking. [43]

Wyndham Council were ordered to reinstate a worker who had been sacked along with four others after they put a private investigator in to spy on a group of Parks staff. [42]

Following this, Victorian MP Bernie Finn demanded that the Council be sacked. [41]

More recently, two Sydney Inner West Council workers were fired for 'bagging the boss' on camera. [40]

Selecting the right candidate ?

What a laugh.

Most Councils proclaim that they always select based on merit alone although of course some do have a policy of promotion within if there are suitable candidates for any vacancy that comes up.

When a new position does become available they advertise, to give everyone the opportunity.

Well actually, in some cases they don't have to, for instance if it's a relatively low level job they can appoint from within the organisation.

Senior employees, however, have specific requirements in order to comply with the Local Government Act. It varies slightly from State to State, but by and large, appointing a senior employee without advertising is not really on. I know of at least one CEO who fell into the role when the previous Chief left, and was subsequently appointed permanently into the role without the job being advertised.

I asked a Councillor why they didn't advertise, and he told me that the acting CEO was doing a good job so there was no need.

Apparently this long time Councillor was unaware of the requirements of the Local Government Act in that regard.

I wonder how many other Councillors are also unaware of the Act.

If it's any consolation, a lot of work has been done in recent years to provide training to newly elected Councillors.

The fiasco at the Joondalup Council which saw the incumbent CEO sacked because he had wrongly claimed qualifications he didn't have, but at least they had advertised the job to recruit, unlike the other example I gave.

Such bullshit goes on and yet I am the one who has found my career going backwards.

I don't know how many positions I have applied for and not been successful but it is now literally dozens.

I have been in the local government game for long enough to know that it is time for something else.

I cannot mentally cope any longer with the level of bullshit that seems to fester in so many of those places.

In some places it's almost as though there are 2 worlds, the fantasy cloud lala land that some senior executive live in, and the harsh under resourced lower ranks, in which the lower level minions get treated with disdainful contempt.

Cheer up, at least you have a job, at least until now, anyway.

Automation is decimating large previous labour intensive sectors, although things are changing rapidly with technology providing solutions which will no doubt change the world in significant ways.

Star Trek were years ahead of the ipad with their hand held computers and their replicator units have beamed into reality with the emergence of 3D printing machines.

Having skills such as craftsmen, or personal services such as dentists or doctors are safe for the time being, but as technology advances, even those traditional professions will increasingly come under threat from robots and computers.

IT related jobs have to be a good one, presumably they will still need people to maintain the computers for some time to come.

Fees and charges?

This hippy looking bloke had walked into my office and proclaimed himself a friend of the Mayor, and then proceeded to tell me he wanted some bins free of charge, because the Mayor said so, and then tried to hand me his mobile because apparently the Mayor was on the phone.

When I refused I explained that there was a process to follow and they wouldn't be getting special treatment just because they were mates with the Mayor.

What a fucking cheek. Forgive me for pointing out the irony for getting my arse kicked – for misusing the internet.

In my experience, the worst part about fees and charges imposed by local governments have been when I have been in a position where I have agreed with a complainant ratepayer, that the fees have been extortionate, justified with some flimsy argument, and all I can suggest is that they put the complaint in writing and request that it be reviewed and/or justified.

Whilst I would have preferred to have been able to say something else, like

"I agree with you, the fees for XYZ are total bullshit. The reasoning behind it is not consistent with industry best practice, the boss is a wanker and just made it up because he apparently has no fucking idea what he is talking about."

But I would have got my arse kicked for that too so I just dealt with the calls, one after the other.

Probably the worst example I can think of, is where a group of hippies were effectively given a piece of land to do their 'community work'.

A nearby resident didn't just telephone or write in, she actually visited me in my office. She had a list of complaints, and one of them was regarding the hippies.

She wanted to know whether the services the hippies were receiving were being properly paid for.

They weren't. I followed up with my boss and his boss and hit a brick wall on the subject.

What happens when the assets are all sold?

Sometimes local governments sell off some major assets like land and property, and then use the money to fund other things, usually other assets that require ongoing funds to maintain.

For example, a Council sells off some commercially valuable land and gets a one off amount of money. That money is used to build a swimming pool which needs staffing and ongoing maintenance and operating expenses.

Whilst the new asset is a positive thing to the community, it has a new swimming pool after all, from another perspective it might be a lost commercial opportunity, especially if the money was spent on something that causes a financial burden on the organisation.

For example, if the land had been retained and leased out on a commercial basis, the asset would still be owned, plus it would be generating an income and with that money a swimming pool could be built just a few years later.

For example at one Council that relocated to another depot, instead of just selling off the site of the old depot, they decided to develop the site and lease it as a commercial property on a 20 year lease with a national retailer.

Sometimes though, the assets that have been owned sometimes for decades, get sold off in order to fund another plaque on the wall.

Consultants galore and contractors even more.

It was happening across the UK a couple of decades before it happened in Australia, but so much land has been flogged off in recent years by local governments, go and check it out and be amazed at how much has gone in the last decade.

At least in Australia, much of the infrastructure is in relatively good condition, compared to say the USA, where much of the ageing infrastructure is now in need of significant repair and/or replacement.

For example, it has been estimated that Americans will need to spend over 1 trillion dollars on municipal water infrastructure by 2025 in order to keep it working.

This shouldn't have come as a surprise, but it seems to me to be a common problem of the past where infrastructure was built, and no or very little consideration was given to whole of life costs, ongoing maintenance requirements and so on.

In many cases, a budget for ad hoc repairs was allocated based on historical needs, rather than for instance building up a reserve account for eventual replacement.

Local municipalities have undoubtedly got much more sophisticated in relation to asset management these days, but there is typically a backlog of already built assets that are going to be very expensive to maintain and replace in the days and years ahead.

In 2016 the Sydney Morning Herald ran an article claiming the NSW Government had sold off 3 Billion dollars of public property. [39]

Also in 2016, the Courier Mail reported on a Queensland Audit Office report which noted that almost half of the 77 Councils were in deficit, with 24 Councils there expecting to be in a deficit position for at least the next decade. [38]

This isn't a new phenomenon, but it's happening in the UK as well, no doubt some of those austerity measures kicking in with massive budget cuts to local governments. [37]

Rates increases

Along with all the other mandatory bills us plebs get to pay, Rates have rocketed up in recent years and there is no sign of this trend ending anytime soon, unless of course by some miracle I get the job, because I would work towards a zero rates goal.

This would be achieved by commercialisation of under-utilised resources and assets already owned. Until that happens, your rates are going up, up and away.

Again this is all part of the UN driven agenda, since they have identified that land ownership is the predominant method that the masses have acquired wealth and ultimately the global governance model seeks control over all the land.

According to the ABS, in the year 2000 the total rates charges in Australia across all Councils totalled about 6 billion dollars per year.

By 2014, this had increased to 15 billion dollars per year.

There is still more space on those office walls to put some expensive plaques and awards on.

One of the biggest cost increases in recent years has been the rise in waste management costs, particularly the disposal and processing costs, and much of this has come about due to the imposition of waste levies for every tonne of waste disposed of to landfill.

In Western Australia, the waste levy charge started out at around $3 per tonne and by 2008 had risen to $8 per tonne. Bear in mind that the State Government were generating over 40 million dollars per year when it was at $3 per tonne.

In 2009 it jumped from $8 per tonne to $28 per tonne. By 2015 it had doubled to $55 per tonne with the promise that it would rise a further $5 per tonne up to 2020.

The worst part about this particularly levy was that when it was originally applied, 50 percent of the total funds raised was put back into waste management, but as the levy increased, the percentage of the funds that went back into waste management decreased to 25%.

The only possible conclusion from this was that the State Government were putting the extra funds back into general revenue.

According to the New Daily, the Council in Australia with the highest taxes is the Gold Coast Council in Queensland, with rates at over $3,200 per year. Victoria had 6 out of 10 of the highest charging local governments in the nation. [36]

Interestingly a comparison between Australia and 7 other developed nations shows that Aussies are taxed more than just about anyone else and Rates are just another one of the long list of taxes that we pay every day. [35]

Widening pay gaps

The gap between what senior executives get and what the rest of the minions get is widening in many cases.

This mirrors what is happening in the private sector although to be fair, the pay levels for a Senior Executive in Local Government typically gets paid a lot less than their private sector counterparts, and certainly much less than the CEO at Australia post who hit the news with his 5 million dollar package.

It seems to me that the lower ranks are being increasingly squeezed.

I recently worked at a Council where the CEO, on a salary of over $250,000 per year, was granted a 3.5% pay increase, and then wanted to pay the staff 2.5 percent.

The justification used was that they couldn't afford to pay and that the CEO had already missed out on a pay rise the previous year.

The Herald Sun reported that in Victoria, Council Chief Executive Officers were earning up to $170,000 per year more than the State Premier, including one CEO listed as earning $460,000 per year. [34]

It's the same story in Western Australia, with Perth Now reporting that 18 local government Chiefs were earning more than the State Premier. [33]

I suppose in the big scheme of things that the widening pay gap issue isn't unique to local governments and I believe that this is all a part of the broader agenda, to effectively eliminate the middle class.

We have plenty of evidence that is the plan, and if one looks closer into the mindset of the privileged class it's not difficult to come to the conclusion that they want a devolved form of humans, the worker class masses, no middle class and the ruling class.

The increased costs of everything are pushing more and more people into poverty, as more of the average pay packet goes into just paying the bills, whilst those that are stacking up the cash get to do more of the same.

The dictatorship

Some Councils have turned into new world order slave camps already.

From what I have seen in such places, the outside workforce is unhappy and subjected to increased levels of tyranny which just gets more and more intrusive and dictatorial as time marches on.

I'm sure there are plenty of people who do work for good municipalities, who enjoy their work and are treated well.

Maybe it's just that I am not friends with any in that category.

As I see it, the worst aspect of the fact that we seem to be marching to the waiting arms of tyranny the world over, at the mercy of decrees from unelected administrators via the various tentacles of the United Nations, is the people who blindly accept the latest outrageous intrusion, and then go one step further and start justifying it with comments like 'Well, ive got nothing to hide.' Dummies, unless they wake up soon they are going to end up being surveilled and tracked 24 hours a day and taxed for the air they breathe via that old Rothschild carbon con.

The United Nations is the vehicle that they have been driving to implement global governance, and the organisation itself founded by club Lucifer and a total and utter farce.

The United Nations has never achieved its stated goals, in fact one could argue it has largely failed miserably and should be disbanded.

At local government level, how many people know that local government had to take steps to try to get recognised in the constitution?

Presumably the reason for that is all those crazy conspiracy theorists who claimed that local governments were not legitimate had a point, perhaps?

Obviously if there was a provision in there already, it wouldn't have been worth making the effort would it?

Fortunately at a local level, there is something that can be done about it, you can put yourself up to get elected onto the Council in order to have a say and these days elected members generally get paid quite well as well.

A solution?

I am sure there are already advocacy groups and the like which help individuals with matters relating to their own local government, so I wont be doing that. However, I along with some other colleagues are aware of just how many people out there are currently having issues with their own dictatorship and so one idea we had was that we could put up a blog, maybe a facebook page and try to help.

Obviously local government workers are still generally quite well unionised, and we aren't qualified to advise on legal matters, but the unions do generally have legal advice support.

That's one part solution for those who still have to endure working at one of the many dysfunctional local governments out there, although it seems to me that unions don't have the same clout they once had.

Local Governments do care about what you say about them, especially if it's on social media, whilst staff aren't able to vent their issues on social media, residents can and increasingly do.

Local Governments can also use social media to highlight all the good things that they are doing.

Triple M radio ran a feature on a Shire of Moora video which went viral, with millions of views of a road surfacing project and this highlighted how local governments can use social media to show people what they are doing effectively. [32]

Over on Facebook there are more than a few groups set up, unofficial pages and groups featuring many local councils, some of them centred around complaints.

As always with Facebook, there's plenty of sarcasm and wit in relation to customer feedback, and over on Youtube, there are some extreme examples of what happens in Council chambers across the world.

Social media is undoubtedly one recent technology which can also provide an improvement in performance and outcomes from your local government, and possibly one of the best solutions moving forwards.

Experiences of some others

Imagine having worked your way up through an organisation, spent 25 years working there and then be told that your position is being downgraded and your new boss is getting upgraded, so you can either take it or voluntarily take redundancy.

That's just one of the few people I know who have also had a rough time whilst working in local government.

I was recently speaking to another local government veteran who had more than 30 years' experience working for local governments. In his most recent role, he was given a car.

The limitation on his private use was that the car could only be used within a 100 km radius of the workplace. One weekend he made multiple trips, all less than 100km.

He was questioned about this 'excessive' use of the vehicle. The vehicle was being tracked with GPS technology, and the result was that he had private use of the car revoked.

He didn't have a car of his own, so each morning one of his team would get in the car, drive from work to his home, and chauffeur him to work. At the end of the day again another team member would drive him home, return the car to work and park it there overnight.

He quit the job, saying that in 30 years of working for local governments, he had never endured such insanity before.

But far more common are people who have had a tough time as a resident dealing with their local government.

A writer at the 'Blacktown Advocate' wrote in 2013

' I HAVE lived in Blacktown for the past 38 years.

I would have to say that this present council is the worst we have ever had in Blacktown.

Selling off council assets which belong to the ratepayers, stopping the pensioner rebate..'

A Gold Coast worker was sacked in 2013 after he raised concerns about public toilets and contacted Councillors to help get some action. [31]

Latrobe City Council employee Alan Cox claimed he was sacked and the sacking was linked to whistleblowing. The issue was eventually resolved, behind closed doors. [30]

It seems to me that there have been numerous examples of where allegations are made and the outcome or conclusion is effectively kept quiet, presumably to preserve the reputation of the organisation or individuals within an organisation.

The more I ask people, the more actual examples I am given.

I have one correspondent who summed it up nicely, in his own words:

'Working for local government is a head fuck. It's as simple as that.'

Another said I was welcome to share his experiences, but I want to get this published and his list is growing by the week.

One resident's subdivision nightmare

In the Port City of Fremantle, one resident spent about 20 years fighting against his local Council, after subdividing his block of land. The problems stemmed from the height of the house which was built, blocking some of his views of the ocean.

Jan Ter Horst was so incensed that he covered his house in graffiti and placed a coffin on the top of his car and emblazoned slogans all over it claiming council corruption. The coffin was apparently referring to the perceived 'death of democracy'.

29

Other Municipalities

Well it doesn't take much research to find some interesting stories from local governments both at home and around the world.

I suppose that because there are so many municipalities it is inevitable that there would be some examples of some that have got into hot water.

The UK and Australia have approximately 1,000 local governments between them, so the fact that I can find dozens of examples of wrongdoing needs to be put into that perspective that there are so many municipalities, on a percentage basis there aren't that many who have done anything wrong.

According to the Western Australian Premier Colin Barnett, he believed that local governments were the 'main source' of corruption. [4]

Sometimes it's the work of an individual and sometimes there are several officials implicated, but the common theme is, wherever you look around the world there are many examples.

I thought about looking further afield, to see whether municipalities in other nations experienced similar issues to those locally.

One of the first I found was a story about a Council in Tehran that had got caught up in a corruption scandal involving real estate. [1]

Over in the USA there was the Bell City scandal involving graft and corruption 2

Over East, in Australia, Maitland residents were shocked to find that the Council were exposed to potential lawsuits which revolved around payments to developers 3

Elsewhere in Australia, the Exmouth Shire sacked the CEO following a CCC investigation 5 and this lead to the Minister for Local Government to begin the process of suspending the whole Council.

In Victoria, the Victorian Ombudsman found that too many councils were shutting the public out from meetings 28

In Ballarat, an ex Councillor was charged with over 40 charges involving an alleged $130,000. 27

In Logan City, a Councillor was charged over an alleged $180,000 theft. 26

The above are all recent news stories relating to local governments, and a look back over the past decade shows this isn't just a few isolated cases. In 2008, Crikey published a summary of some of the Councils it termed the 'dodgiest Councils' 25

Brimbank City Council were sacked in 2009 following a variety of inappropriate misconduct allegations against elected members 24

In 2013 the Wangaratta Council was sacked following allegations of bullying and intimidating behaviour 23

Between 2012 and 2014 the Canning Council was suspended with the eventual sacking of all elected members due to a massive report conducted by the Department of Local Government which cited widespread dysfuntion amongst other issues. 22

More recently in Tasmania, the Huon Valley Council in 2016, following allegations of problems with transparency and accountability 21

Perth City Council sacked the CEO in 2016 and the State opposition leader said he would sack the Mayor. 20

Whilst the list in this section is by no means comprehensive, I hope it shows that wrongdoings by Councils isn't something that hardly ever happens. Quite the opposite it would seem.

I also make the point again that there are many local governments that have never been found guilty of any wrongdoing, so perhaps your Council is one of the good ones.

The worst of it

In 2015, Latrobe City Council called the police over a suspected 2 million dollar fraud case involving one individual who had allegedly done so over a period of twelve years. 19

In 2016 a researcher looking into local government in Sydney is quoted as saying in conclusion that "I think there is a lot of corruption that's occurring that is not being reported and I don't say that lightly because I'm passionate about local government."18

Also in 2016, the Washington Post ran an article entitled 'This might be the most corrupt little town in America.' The article cited about 200 investigations conducted by the FBI over the previous two years involving alleged corruption. 17

Also in the USA, one blogger resident of Jefferson county posted about 'piss poor management' of his local municipality. 16

Over at NYmag.com, Jonathan Chait zoomed in on Ferguson in an article entitled 'Why the Worst Governments in America are Local Governments.' In the article he zoomed in on Ferguson, and said:

'*The town of Ferguson, while tiny in scale, is an Orwellian monstrosity. Its racially biased Police Department is the enforcement wing of a predatory system of government described in scathing detail in a recent report by ArchCity Defenders, a Missouri legal-aid nonprofit.'* 15

Over in the UK there is a website called rottencouncil.co.uk which details a list of complaints focusing on planning issues. 14

The Development and Environmental Professionals' Association ran article entitled 'Who has the worst HR in local government in 2015' and it listed more than a few candidates in the article, with issues ranging from industrial disputes to salary structuring. 13

In 2016 the ABC ran an article on the City of Kalgoorlie Boulder following its ranking as one of the most financially unhealthy councils in the State. The article quoted the Council as needing to take 'ruthless austerity measures' as a result. 12

Complaints to local governments

In my own experience, most complaints made to local governments are relatively minor issues.

The most common issues include things like:

- Noise complaints – often from neighbouring businesses or residents making loud noise at inappropriate times, such as late at night or early in the morning
- Rubbish complaints – such as litter, illegally dumped waste, missed bin collections
- Parks and tree complaints – such as trees that need pruning, parks that need mowing or maintenance
- Street maintenance issues – graffiti, broken or damaged street furniture
- Complaints about administrative issues such as planning, Council decisions

The above probably constitute the vast majority of complaints received by most local governments, although they are generally labelled as 'customer requests' rather than complaints.

Sometimes however the 'customer requests' escalate to complaints when the issue remains unresolved.

When Comedian Eugene Mirman parked his car and paid for three hours of parking and then got a parking ticket, he wrote a reply and went even further by arranging to publish the letter in a local publication.

11

Moreton Bay Regional Council reportedly wanted a local towing business to move their shop half a metre due to zoning issues, despite the business having been there for decades. 10

In Norwich, a resident complained to the Ombudsman after a drainage issue damaged the wall to her property and remained unresolved until the Ombudsman stepped in and in ordered the Council to pay for half the cost of the repairs. 9

It is amazing though how many times I have personally dealt with issues that really relate to one neighbour complaining about the other.

On many of those occasions I have ended up suggesting the radical notion of talking to their neighbour instead of me about their issue.

But it is remarkable how many people out there want their local council tie their shoelaces for them, and when informed that isn't a service currently provided by the Council, they have often remarked that it should.

Perhaps it's an indication of how docile and apathetic society has become towards government generally, although perhaps this is changing, we have a long way to go to get to the point where the general populace takes more of an active interest in how we are governed.

How does your Council perform?

Some places have got websites that compare local governments. In Western Australia for example you can go to http://knowyourcouncil.com

The site has a number of ways you can compare Councils with some key data.

Obviously there are vast differences between the rate base and area covered, so caution could be suggested when comparing, but for instance if you wanted to compare two local councils both in the same metropolitan area and with similar demographics it could be handy.

The big question as to how your council performs is likely to be one you already have your own opinion on. I think the important questions to ask include 'Does my Council spend the money appropriately?' How does your Council spend it? Is it well managed? Is the infrastructure well managed, or are there examples of things that have been built and fallen into disrepair?

Smile, you're on camera

It's not just the cameras on the street that watch what's going on, many local councils record their meetings, and social media is full of examples of some behaviour which supports my view that it can be a ride into crazy town.

Hudson Council USA shouting match went on youtube 6

Another American slanging match "you're all a disgrace" 7

Over in the UK, it's fisticuffs at Briercliffe 8

Believe you can make a difference

Sometimes, when local governments make a decision that a lot of people don't like, I have seen first hand how a small vocal minority can get a decision reversed.

I saw this happen in a City with about 10,000 households, where a vocal minority that totalled no more than 130 people applied enough pressure to force a back track on the decision.

Remember that at the end of the day, local Government is the level of Government which is closest to the people, and for that reason alone is one which provides the ability to respond rapidly to resident wishes, but we have to let them know that we will be there, holding their feet to the flame as required, so that we can get the right outcomes.

The End

Well when you put it all together, how's it looking so far?

I have really just rattled off thousands of words at a rate of knots because I just had to get this off my chest and having completed that task, I can now continue on feeling better about the fact I have had my say.

I would also like to make the point that I could have gone on and on and on with news stories relating to local governments that I came across when researching the topic, but I think I have given enough examples to make the point.

Take more interest in your local government.

You have an elected representative who can champion your cause if you need action.

There is often a greater priority placed on to requests that have come from an elected member than other complaints and requests, so if you are having a problem with your local council, try contacting the Councillor for your area.

Thanks for reading.

References

1 http://www.al-monitor.com/pulse/originals/2016/08/tehran-city-council-real-estate-ghalibaf-chamran.html

2 https://en.wikipedia.org/wiki/City_of_Bell_scandal

3 http://www.maitlandmercury.com.au/story/4256751/council-scandal-exposes-lawsuit/?cs=2452

4   http://www.perthnow.com.au/news/western-australia/barnett-local-councils-the-main-source-of-corruption-in-wa/news-story/4320dfd523a5aacd2828c99ee6aba543

5   http://www.abc.net.au/news/2016-12-16/sacked-shire-of-exmouth-ceo-apologises-to-community/8127448

6   https://www.youtube.com/watch?v=EPfvLKPW3ro

7   https://www.youtube.com/watch?v=rFeA-pM0o8Y

8   https://www.youtube.com/watch?v=Tm0NDisosB8

9 http://www.edp24.co.uk/news/politics/norwich_city_council_told_it_must_pay_part_of_cost_to_rebuild_woman_s_wall_after_complaint_to_watchdog_1_4843126

10

http://www.cabooolturenews.com.au/news/rudds-towing-takes-on-council-in-david-and-goliath/3135479/

11

http://www.dearcustomerrelations.com/2015/09/eugene-mirman-parking-complaint/

12 http://www.abc.net.au/news/2016-05-02/kalgoorlie-bolder-council-one-of-worst-financial-managers-wa/7377436

13 http://www.depa.net.au/news-a-views/latest-news/351-who-has-the-worst-hr-in-local-government-in-2015.html

14 https://www.rottencouncil.co.uk/complaints/

15
http://nymag.com/daily/intelligencer/2014/09/ferguson-worst-governments.html

16 https://gesvol.wordpress.com/2009/07/14/worst-local-government-ever/

17

https://www.washingtonpost.com/world/national-security/this-might-be-the-most-corrupt-little-town-in-america/2016/03/05/341c21d2-dcac-11e5-81ae-7491b9b9e7df_story.html?utm_term=.7fd79c866084

18
http://www.governmentnews.com.au/2016/12/corrupti
on-investigations-at-auburn-hurstville-and-rockdale-
councils-the-tip-of-the-iceberg-says-researcher/

19 http://www.heraldsun.com.au/news/law-
order/latrobe-city-council-hit-by-2m-fraud-
claims/news-
story/1fef1810bc84a5a46bdc0144656f2f98

20 http://www.communitynews.com.au/guardian-
express/news/opposition-leader-mcgowan-calls-on-
state-govt-to-sack-city-of-perth-council/

21 http://www.news.com.au/national/breaking-
news/southern-tasmanian-council-sacked/news-
story/1387970c85be34562024dac502428495

22 http://www.watoday.com.au/wa-news/take-two-
canning-council-sacked-again-commissioners-
appointed-20140916-10hrpr.html

23 http://www.theage.com.au/victoria/wangaratta-
council-sacked-over-toxic-culture-20130918-
2ty76.html

24 http://www.heraldsun.com.au/news/brimbank-city-
council-sacked-by-state-government/news-
story/f38158d48c3e090321b84deb4eda4a25

25 https://www.crikey.com.au/2008/03/04/australias-
dodgiest-local-councils-a-crikey-list/

26 http://www.abc.net.au/news/2016-12-15/stealing-charge-logan-councillor-stacey-mcintosh-stands-down/8124332

27 http://www.abc.net.au/news/2016-12-15/lukas-carey-allegedly-defrauded-ballarat-council/8124684

28 http://www.abc.net.au/news/2016-12-16/victorian-public-shut-out-of-local-council-meetings-ombudsman/8126542

29 https://www.google.com.au/search?q=jan+ter+horst&client=firefox-b&tbm=isch&imgil=td86FvaVxjy-YM%253A%253BqsR1BBwd7RIvzM%253Bhttp%25253A%25252F%25252Fwww.news.com.au%25252Fnational%25252Fcourt-rules-on-jan-ter-horsts-graffiti-battle%25252Fstory-e6frfkp9-1225764517155&source=iu&pf=m&fir=td86FvaVxjy-YM%253A%252CqsR1BBwd7RIvzM%252C_&usg=__9HSOwAjw0EpAGL1sfS9SlhAeNNs%3D&biw=1366&bih=657&ved=0ahUKEwi-7rrbiMjRAhXKHpQKHWLwCowQyjcITQ&ei=unh9WL6pKsq90ATi4KvgCA#imgrc=td86FvaVxjy-YM%3A

[30] http://www.latrobevalleyexpress.com.au/story/2627714/closure-for-sacked-latrobe-city-whistleblower/

[31] http://www.goldcoastbulletin.com.au/news/council/gold-coast-city-council-whistleblower-shown-the-door-

after-highlighting-poor-contract-cleaners/news-story/6921ec97c311f8e1351eab148fe72fca

[32] https://www.triplem.com.au/news/perth/why-more-wa-councils-should-be-like-the-shire-of-moora/?station=centralwheatbelt

[33] http://www.perthnow.com.au/news/western-australia/new-figures-show-18-local-council-ceos-can-now-earn-more-than-premier-colin-barnett/news-story/f77c79e45594ab77a36bd40d6d8fcf0e

[34] http://www.heraldsun.com.au/news/victoria/victorian-council-bosses-earning-up-to-170000-more-than-premier-daniel-andrews/news-story/268ad58db6b8cb7b618d1f84efb9de05

[35] http://www.movehub.com/advice/tax-comparisons-around-the-world

[36] http://thenewdaily.com.au/money/property/2016/02/17/local-council-gouging-rates-charges/

[37] https://www.theguardian.com/public-leaders-network/2016/nov/18/budget-cuts-councils-assets-quick-buck

[38] http://www.couriermail.com.au/news/queensland/damning-state-audit-office-report-claims-councils-risking-financial-failure/news-story/fc86dd5a6030bb5d9a2f787f43364590

[39] http://www.smh.com.au/nsw/mike-bairds-3-billion-selloff-of-public-buildings-20151231-glxcwu.html

[40] https://au.news.yahoo.com/a/34028151/parking-inspectors-sacked-after-body-camera-records-them-bagging-their-boss/#page1

[41] http://www.news.com.au/national/victoria/politics/victorian-mp-bernie-finn-tells-parliament-wyndham-council-should-be-sacked/news-story/08570fd6ff181ba94c293ba74e741014

[42] http://www.theage.com.au/victoria/wyndham-council-told-to-reinstate-worker-sacked-on-word-of-spy-20131018-2vrb3.html

[43] http://www.themercury.com.au/news/scales-of-justice/sacked-council-worker-claims-age-discrimination/news-story/e6c61dc70cbcb39751a8c4e2d040300a

[44] http://www.abc.net.au/news/2009-07-29/council-workers-sacked-over-free-sandwich/1371772

[45] http://www.news.com.au/finance/work/council-workers-sacked-for-taking-smoko-at-surfers-paradise-pie-shop/news-story/5a3fabdf2f2969244b93fd47cb141d33?pg=1

[46] http://www.chroniclelive.co.uk/news/north-east-news/rogue-newcastle-council-officer-sacked-11968913

[47] http://www.adelaidenow.com.au/news/south-australia/yorke-peninsula-council-finance-manager-karen-maria-schulz-charged-with-60-counts-of-theft-after-icac-investigation/news-story/9b0f9bf9dfb7afbb6ded1b0159662d5a

[48] http://www.smh.com.au/news/national/ratepayers-hit-as-400m-wiped-out/2008/04/02/1206851011851.html

[49] http://www.newstatesman.com/uk-politics/2013/08/nine-spectacular-council-outsourcing-failures

[50] http://www.theage.com.au/victoria/60-million-of-taxpayer-funds-blown-on-failed-project-20160309-gnemfi.html

[51] http://www.ewg.org/agmag/2014/04/extreme-levels-herbicide-roundup-found-food

[52] http://responsibletechnology.org/irtnew/wp-content/uploads/2016/01/2-Glyphosate-Bans-and-Restrictions-Across-the-Globe.pdf